THE VALLEY

PRACTICAL STEPS TO IDENTIFY HOW YOU GOT THERE AND HOW <u>GOD</u> CAN GET YOU OUT

TARRYN SARCONE

Hardcover: 979-8-9890646-0-1
Paperback: 979-8-9890646-1-8
Ebook: 979-8-9890646-2-5

Library of Congress Number: 2023916438
First paperback edition October 2023

Tarrynsarcone.com

To John, my biggest supporter. Thank you for loving me and letting me be me. Without your support, love and encouragement, this book never would've been written simply because I would no longer exist. I love you more.

TABLE OF CONTENTS

FORWARD

From as far back as I can remember, I knew I was chosen. Not in a conceited "I'm better than you" way; it was just an inner knowing that I was set apart and special. I knew God had something big in store for me. (Maybe you can relate.) Although I believed that to my inner core, that didn't mean I was confident, had great self-worth, or was well-liked growing up. I was actually the opposite—always struggling to fit in, acting like someone I wasn't, and desperately throwing myself at men in hopes for their attention, approval, and validation.

My issues with men started as generational sin into my life, and there was nothing I could do to change that. My mom got pregnant with me when she was eighteen and remained in a toxic relationship with my father until I was born. She met another man after I was born, and they got married. I lived with my mom and her husband who then had three additional children. We were a happy traditional American family. I saw my biological dad off and on rarely up until age nine when he signed off his rights as my father and I was adopted by my stepdad (although I never considered him to be a step parent).

He was my dad, and very rarely did I ever even remember he wasn't my blood. Even though I had an amazing dad in my life and was taken care of, loved, and adored, I still felt deep down abandonment by my biological father. When I turned eighteen, I mustered up the courage and sent him an email saying, "Hi! Remember me?" That's all I remember from the email, but still to this day, I think how his heart must have sunk into the pit of his stomach when he came to work the next morning, seeing an email from his daughter who he hadn't seen or heard from in nine years.

We started building a relationship slowly and remained in each other's lives for about a year. Then *poof,* he was gone again.

I stewed in my hatred and anger for him, acting as if I didn't care at all where he went, but when I found out I was pregnant with twins at the age of nineteen, I reached out to him and brought him back into my life again. He remained in our lives for several more years before disappearing again.

Why did he keep disappearing? I had no clue, and it ate me alive to not understand. Was it me? Was I doing something wrong? Was there something wrong with me I'm an analytical person, and my mind immediately goes to solving a problem when presented with one, but I thought of everything, and nothing made sense.

He was back again for baby number three and gone just as quick. I swore in my resentment, unforgiveness, and anger: never again.

I was broken. I felt forgotten, unimportant, thrown away, rejected, small, and unworthy. I let those emotions define me for far too long. I believed it was my identity.

The reason I share all of this is to show you that my problems, like most of us, began even before I was conceived. Most of us are born into generational sins and curses, out of our control, but we must first learn to identify them and begin to work to grow past them in order to heal and move forward with our lives out of bondage. The devil prowls around like a lion waiting for someone to devour, and he most definitely looks for families that he can divide and destroy which will then cause more trauma, wounds, and brokenness.

"Broken" (adj.): Having been fractured or damaged and no longer in one piece and working order.

When using the word "broken" in this sense, it's only based on someone's belief. The only thing Satan is banking on to "win you over" and make your life feel broken is your belief about it. He has no real authority over the children of God.

The Bible says that "The reason the Son of God appeared was to destroy the devil's work" (1 John 3:8 [NIV]). If we go through life believing that we are broken by our sins or circumstances, we will never reach our greatest potential and become who we were created to be.

The way I felt was not who I was. That was not my identity and who God created me to be.

What was I created for? In order to answer this question, I first had to look at my Creator and ask Him. He didn't speak us into existence like everything else He created in the world, but He made us by hand (Genesis 1). We are the only thing He made by hand and formed in His likeness. Which means you and I are magnificent, unique, and wonderful miracles on earth because God had a purpose for us and a plan for our life—as He said, "For I know the plans I have for you, plans to give you hope and a future" (Jeremiah 29:11).

Maybe you don't quite believe what God has to say about you yet, but the devil does. That's why he is going to try to do anything he can to get you off of your destined path for greatness.

Although I knew deep, deep down that I was created by God for something big, from a young age, I also could tell there was a battle happening over my life daily. For a long time, I let the devil trick me into believing his lies that I was broken. Actually, he had me believing some lies this morning that crept back up. He was telling me that I am a nobody, that writing this book will never make an impact and that I'll never finish because I've never finished anything in my life, so I should just give up now. But when I began thinking this, I immediately phoned a friend and she turned the lights onto the devil's schemes (more on this later).

Satan hates the light. He doesn't want us to walk in the light; he wants to keep us in dark pits with him, thinking we're all alone, that nobody else wants to hear about our struggles. He wants us to sulk in our own misery. When we feel like this, most of us isolate, binge-watch Netflix shows, lay in bed all day, ignore text messages, DMs, and phone calls. We cancel plans, we yell at our kids, we tell everyone we're "fine," and we reach for anything to feel better in the moment. But if you can see that it's all part of the devil's plan to get you alone with him and off of your mission... Well, then you can fight against him before he even gets started.

This isn't a book condemning you for watching Netflix, taking naps, and indulging in the occasional glass of wine with your friends. Quite the opposite, actually. The culture we live in tells us to hustle and sacrifice, and if we lay around, we're lazy. Some of you never stop moving, while others have a hard time finding the motivation to get moving. We all have our own demons and chains and vices—we're all the same, even if we seem so different. By the end of this book, I'm going to show you how to deal with all your struggles, whatever they may be.

You are chosen and anointed to do great things. You are set apart, and God has a plan for your life. Yes, *you*. If this is hard to believe, it's because you've been abused into doubt. The way you grew up, how you treated yourself, the things people have said to you and done to you, the ways they have mistreated you, labeled you, and abandoned you have made you think this way. You currently act *exactly* as someone who experienced the life you have experienced would act. You are not crazy, or messed up, or a failure. You are not too far gone for hope. There is always hope for the future in Christ.

In order to create a life of pure joy and fulfillment, I had to learn my true identity, but first I had to unlearn and remove all of the labels that had been placed on me so far in life, and in their place, put on all the truths that God designed me to be. That is what we will focus on learning first. By the way, the only person who can define and say what something is, is The Creator of it.

The devil is jealous of us because of how much God loves us and hates him, so he constantly is trying to tempt us, deceive us, and lure us into thinking that our ways are better than God's ways. The devil wants us to believe that things of this world are the things that really matter. He is going to try to mess with your identity, calling, passions, purpose, family, focus, confidence, purity, rest, and contentment. It is a constant tug-of-war battle for your life. How precious a soul must be for two forces to be after it.

But I have good news! God has already defeated the devil, and He has won! If we are on God's team, if we are on mission for Him and what He values, then nothing is impossible.

I am writing this book out of pain and purpose, with the urgency in my heart to rescue you from the deepest pit of the Valley. I know what it's like to live there for way too long, and I know exactly what it feels like to feel hopeless and helpless and miserable all at the same time. I know you want to be happy. I know you want to feel fulfilled. I know you think you're too messed up for God to help, especially with all the sins in your life that you keep running back to. I know you don't feel worthy—you have so much shame and guilt shackled to your ankles, pulling you down because of things you've done in your past that it seems impossible to ever be free.

But I want to ask you a question: Do you want to be well? This is a question Jesus asked the man at the pool in Bethesda who was paralyzed for 38 years. This pool was a place where a lot of disabled people used to lay—the blind, the lame, and the paralyzed—in hopes for a miracle. Legend said that when the bubbles started to form in the pool, if you were the first one in the water, you would be healed. Imagine being so desperate for help, so desperate for a miracle, that you held onto a legend and sat by a pool for years, just hoping that one day you would be healed. That man did exactly that, even though it was impossible for him to even get to the pool, since he was paralyzed.

Put yourself in this man's place for just one minute. He endured 38 years of suffering and desperation. How long have you been suffering for? Since birth? Since that last relationship that left you empty and feeling worthless? Since that job that sucked the life out of you? Since your partner left you? Since your loved one died? Since your addiction began? Since the first time you were abused? Since the affair began? Since the diagnosis?

When Jesus saw him lying there, He asked him, "Do you want to get well?"

"Sir," the man replied, "I have no one to help me into the pool when the water is stirred. While I am trying to get in, someone else goes down ahead of me."

(Notice his logical thinking, mindset and excuses... Sound familiar?)

This is my favorite part of the scripture in John 5... "Then Jesus said to him, 'Get up! Pick up your mat and walk.' At once the man was cured; he picked up his mat and walked away."

Jesus can and will heal your brokenness. Psalm 34:18 says, "The Lord is close to the brokenhearted and saves those who are crushed in spirit." But the question remains, do you want to be well? If you answered yes, then you're ready for what lies ahead in this book. I am going to teach you how to expose the devil in your life, learn who your creator says you are, tap into your individual identity, talents and gifts. We're going to begin the healing process of the trauma and abuse you have endured and the coping mechanisms you have formed to help you protect yourself. You are going to learn how to recognize your triggers and learn to create a proactive vs. a reactive life for your family. Most importantly, I am going to teach you how to stay connected to God in order to co-create your life, living and walking daily hand-in-hand, side-by-side with our father.

You see, nothing—and I mean nothing—will ever satisfy you like Jesus will. The drugs get old after a while, so does the alcohol, the shopping, the people-pleasing, and sex with strangers. The money never feels as good as you think it will, the success won't bring you the joy and fulfillment that you long for. We're not actually after "the thing." What we're really after is the feeling we get when we achieve "the thing." Having $10,000 in your bank account is just a number in a bank account. But it's what you could do with the $10,000 that's exciting, the freedom it could offer you, the stuff you could buy with it, but when the money's gone, the feeling is gone too. What if I could tell you that you could get that feeling and never lose it again no matter how much money is in your account? That you could find your purpose in the pain, passion for your life ahead and a calling on your life that's so divine, and so rich it has you coming back for more day after day.

I know you're tired. I know you feel like you can't keep doing this, and on some days, you've thought about ending it all. I know, because I was you. Life seems so hard right now and everything seems like it's sinking. If you bought this book, I bet your mental health is pretty poor right now, I would bet that your physical health is also declining pretty rapidly too. Your energy levels are low, you're not eating the way you want to eat, and you're not sleeping very well at night either. Even if you do get a full eight hours of sleep, you're waking up feeling exhausted. Your marriage or intimate relationships probably aren't thriving either, because how can they when you're constantly triggered, overwhelmed, sad, and stressed out? You hate yourself, you have poor body image, and you have a hard time recognizing anything about yourself that you like. You're also over-sensitive and extremely emotional.

If you have children, they're probably out of control too, you feel overwhelmed at just the thought of getting out of bed in the morning to do another day and the anger and rage that's billowing up inside of you is already giving you mom guilt. You want to run away and disappear from life but can't actually imagine doing it. You know how the day is going to go because nothing has changed in years no matter how hard you try. You have poor boundaries, you are a people-pleaser and you rarely say no to things unless your kids ask. You wish you were a fun mom, the mom who runs in the sprinkler with her kids in the summer or buys the balloons and has a water balloon fight. Instead, you're the mom thinking what a mess that will make and all you want to do is crawl into bed. I would bet that you haven't taken a lot of time to spend with friends lately either. What started as ignoring their texts and calls has turned into full out isolation and avoidance because "nobody wants me around them when I feel like this."

The devil has done a good job at destroying your life one thing at a time and getting you to think the absolute worst of yourself. That's his job. He wants you to think that you can do life without God, that God doesn't know best. He wants you to think you're in control and he tricks us into thinking that everything else, other than God, will make us feel good again. He is a liar. He is the father of all lies and nothing that comes out of his mouth or from him is good.

I promise, if you read this book and apply these principles to your life, you will, without a doubt, feel renewed, restored, and alive. How do I know that? Because of God. I'm not writing this book. God is using me to write it and I've prayed for years that the people He wants to read it will end up with it in their hands (or audible accounts). In fact, this is the very next breadcrumb in your life that God has left for you (more about "breadcrumbs" later). He hears you, He sees your sadness, and He is answering your prayers right now. You didn't find this book by accident or by random coincidence. It is a divine direction for your life. He is speaking to you, He hears your cries, He knows your heart, and He is ready to open the flood gates and pour peace, love, and abundance into you.

Bottom line. You are not alone. You are not crazy, you are not your past, you are not who people have said you are—you are Chosen and Anointed. You are a child of the Most High King who is head-over-heels in love with you and wants you healed and well so that you can live out your purpose while on earth to feel fulfilled, joyful, and free...

Do you want to be well?

If so, let's begin our time together with a prayer: "God, thank you for connecting me to this book and knowing the desires of my heart. Help the words in this book connect to my soul. Lower the walls that guard my heart and allow the Holy Spirit to speak to me. Help me to finish this book and not get distracted by creating an urgency in my soul to continue reading everyday so that I can consume every ounce of goodness you have for me. Thank you for being with me in my life every step of the way, even if I didn't acknowledge your presence. Help me to become the person you created me to be. Amen."

PART ONE

DESCENDING

THE VALLEY

It was August 26th, 2020 and I locked myself in my bathroom, crying hysterically after just snapping at my kids. It was a time in my life where I had achieved everything I ever wanted and had everything that money could buy, but yet I felt the worst I have ever felt. I was bent over my sink hyperventilating, cursing the devil for attacking me with this depression and anxiety, desperately waiting for a reply back from the text message I sent my husband John that said, "I just can't do this anymore... it's too much." And that's when it happened. It was the very first time I heard God speak to me, but it was also the first time I felt His presence physically in the same room as me too.

The voice wasn't an audible voice that boomed from the sky in an almighty authoritative tone, but instead it was my own voice inside my head, but it wasn't my own thought or even said in my own current emotion. While crying and hunched over the sink, I felt someone standing behind me. Instantly, I stopped crying and just froze. As I stared blankly into the sink I heard, "You are chosen and anointed.

Your anxiety and depression is not from the devil but from yourself. The further you get from me, the more distractions you welcome into your life, the worse you will feel. Draw near to me every day and your anxiety and depression will go away. Share what you're learning, be vulnerable and tell people your story. You're stronger than you think."

I looked up to the mirror, certain someone was standing behind me, but no one was there. I turned around, thinking the mirror was playing tricks on me, but it wasn't. Nobody was there, except the feeling was still present. It was the most amazing, comforting feeling I have ever felt in my entire life. Just writing about the experience brings tears of joy to my eyes seeing now how much God was with me through every anxiety attack, every struggle and every tear. He heard my prayers and cries for help and He showed up, and I know that He will do the same for you.

"When the righteous cry for help, the Lord hears and delivers them out of all their troubles" (Psalm 34:17).

I picked up the closest notebook and wrote down what I had just heard, desperate to never forget the words and instructions God spoke over me that day.

Now, I wasn't a stranger to God. I was raised Catholic, was baptized and attended mass on Easter and Christmas, and I completed catechism and made my first communion. We were the type of people who just did what everyone else did. We went to church occasionally and followed the traditions and rituals, having no idea what they meant, but we did it because that's what my grandma did and that's what her mom did too. Religion to us was about rules, limitations, and condemnation. It had nothing to do with a personal relationship with Jesus. We never experienced Him and didn't really understand or know His character either.

When I was twelve, my mom started searching for answers and wanted to know more about God, the Bible, and how to live a life of fulfillment and purpose, so she began "church-hopping" on Sundays until she finally found a church that felt like home to her. That year, she was baptized in a river with my aunt and they gave their lives to the Lord by admitting they were sinners. They couldn't get to heaven without Jesus, and that they believed He died on the cross for their sins. I was water-baptized several years later, right before my 16th birthday.

Now, I wish I could tell you that we all lived happily ever after and the devil never attacked us again, but I have a different story to share. I was a very rebellious child, very strong-willed, very manipulative, also trying to heal wounds of abandonment and rejection the best I knew how as a teenager.

I reached for acceptance in men particularly but also with "friends" at school, wanting to desperately fit in and to be accepted. I did anything to look cool, and also clung onto things like alcohol and popularity as my idols that made me feel whole and happy (in the moment).

You'll hear me use the word idol a lot in this book, so here's what it means: Anything we treasure more than God—whatever drives our actions and thoughts becomes an idol. These idols dull our spiritual hearing and harden our hearts to things of God. Idolatry isn't just worshiping false gods, but it's so much more. You can idolize yourself, your security, approval from others, relationships, achieving success, wealth, health, food, intellect, comfort, and the list goes on.

As a young adult, the brokenness and insecurity turned from fake friends, popularity, and the occasional drunken night at a party to an insatiable need for the approval of men. I also swapped out the occasional drunken night to get as drunk as I could five out of seven nights a week, and when that stopped numbing my pain, I turned to smoking weed, snorting cocaine, and taking any pill I could get my hands on. When I was drunk, high, or having sex with a stranger, I felt fun. I felt adventurous, desired, wanted, funny, happy, excited, loud, confident, secure, free, and numb. Numbness was the biggest reason I was escaping to this fantasy life daily so that I wouldn't have to deal with the pain of my wounds caused by my abandonment as a child.

What are your wounds? What do you escape from and how do you escape from it? Do you max out your credit cards? Compulsively shop at stores or have new brown Amazon boxes showing up on your front porch daily? Do you overeat? Do you put up walls and push people out of your life when you feel threatened or rejected or you fear you're about to be? Is it a hidden pill addiction? We all have something. It's just like sinning. We were all born with sin and wounds and we all want, more than anything, to just feel better.

The world tells us that all the things mentioned above will make us feel better, and the sad thing is we believe that they will, but I promise you, they will eventually become chains on your ankles and keep you bound from all the goodness God has for you. You will become a prisoner of the devil, chained to your addiction, your hurt, your trauma, and your soul will die down in the Valley. You will cause generational sin and curses to continue throughout your generations if you have children. You will cause wounds and traumas in your children that you never would do intentionally but find yourself at a loss of how to stop it from happening. If you can't do this for yourself, do it for them. And if you're not a parent, do it for your future children so that they don't have to grow up with a mom or dad who is broken and hurt.

I first began talking about this term "Valley" a couple years ago when I started journaling about my own mental health after some self-help books suggested it. After reading several scriptures referencing the peaks and valleys of a mountain and comparing it to life, I realized it wasn't a lull that I was in... I was in a Valley. I noticed that when I was in a Valley, I would experience the same emotions and thoughts and behavioral patterns and all of them were negative. My mind would race with worry, and it was like everyone and everything was demanding my attention and I felt like I was screaming for help, but no matter how loud I screamed, nobody could hear me over all of the noise. I was surrounded by people but felt completely alone.

And my poor husband. That sweet man did everything he could for me but had no idea how to help me. He's the type of person who is analytical, very matter-of-fact, black and white, right or wrong, and has no mental health issues whatsoever and could not relate to me in the slightest bit. But he had seen me struggle for years, including the last year when it had become the absolute worst. He would come home from work and find me crying somewhere in the house, sleeping, drinking, smoking, coping in any way that I could to just feel better in that moment. I remember lying in bed while he stood at the door and I was bawling, saying over and over again, "I just want to be happy. I just want to be happy." He had no idea how to help but he was as patient as he could be, which most times wasn't patient enough for me, which caused me to spiral even deeper into my depression, isolation, and mental sickness, feeling like I was crazy and completely alone in my struggle, which is one of the biggest lies I've seen Satan try to trick us with, and the very lie that is fueling me to write this book. We are not alone in this struggle! More people can relate to brokenness than they can to wholeness.

Your spouse is not the problem. Your finances are not the problem. Your job is not the problem. The main problem is that you are stuck in the Valley and don't know how to get out. Once you get out, all of the other problems begin to work themselves out but we can't do anything in our own power. We have to first admit that we are power-less to change in our own strength.

"I know that nothing good lives in me, that is, in my flesh; for I have the desire to do what is good, but I cannot carry it out" (Romans 7:18).

You need Jesus to carry you out of the Valley just like He carried me. You cannot do this alone anymore. How has it been going so far doing this thing called life in your own strength?

Journaling

How do you feel right now as a result of the experiences and choices you have made so far in life? On a scale of one to ten, how fulfilled do you feel? How free do you feel? How much joy do you experience in the sober parts of your life? Go ahead, grab a notebook and rate yourself. In fact, why don't you get yourself a blank, brand-new note-book that we can write some things in during the time frame of you reading this book. It doesn't have to be anything fancy, it just has to be blank. Today, you might give yourself sevens straight across the board, but do this exercise again next week while you're in a deep Valley and you'll give yourself ones and twos. Sometimes I would do this and give myself zeroes or even negative numbers. This is exactly how I felt emo-tionally on the day I journaled about wanting to end my own life. The valleys are low and the peaks are high. The reason I started journaling was to remember the darkness that filled my mind once I got out of it. I didn't want to forget how dark it was.

When I would journal, I would place a little arrow at the top right corner that either pointed up, or it pointed down. This showed where my mind was on that day and it helped me to begin tracking patterns in my life. When I began recognizing the warning signs of the Valley, I felt like I could finally start to make sense of it.

Awareness

I believe I lived in my first Valley until just a few weeks after my encounter with God. So, for the majority of my life, I was in the same Valley because I never recognized where I had taken up my permanent residence. I developed this "Oh well, this is my life" kind of attitude. Like, "These were the cards I was dealt," or "I'll just live like this forever" type of mentality.

Once I got out of the Valley for the first time, I had this overwhelming amount of joy. This was a Joy where I couldn't stop smiling, I couldn't stop singing, and my eyes filled with tears because I couldn't believe how grateful I was for even the smallest things in my life. I remember looking at my kitchen that night before going to bed and seeing toys and clothes and messes everywhere. Instead of looking at them with disgust like I had every other night before, I viewed things differently. I started weeping and thanking God for every little hand that left a Barbie, Peppa Pig toy, or book out. I then thanked Him for every person in my family who wore one of the 30 pairs of shoes in the hallway and my heart honestly felt like it was going to explode out of my chest.

Sadly, the feeling only lasted a short while until I was back in the Valley again. Was it possible to get out and stay out? I wasn't sure but I was desperate to find out.

My abandonment issues hurt so bad, and as a young girl, I started doing whatever I could to numb the pain. We will do anything to alleviate it. So instead of feeling rejected, forgotten, and insignificant, I wanted to feel accepted, approved of, adored, loved, and remembered.

When I was a late teen, I began using sex as a coping mechanism and it worked, but it was only temporary. Every encounter with a guy left me feeling more and more broken, so I would go after the feeling even harder, driving me further down into the Valley. It was a terrible time in my life and now looking back to think about it and write it down to share with you makes me so sad for her. I wish more than anything I knew my worth back then, to know how adored I was, how chosen I was, how unique and wonderful I was in God's eyes. It's my hope for you that you find out your worth and never forget it. You might be 18 years old reading this book, 34, or maybe 55 and still struggling. But are you reaching for idols, and coping mechanisms to numb your pain or are you reaching for Jesus?

"Blessed is the man who trusts in the Lord, whose trust is the Lord. He is like a tree planted by water, that sends out its roots by the stream, and does not fear when heat comes, for its leaves remain green, and is not anxious in the year of drought, for it does not cease to bear fruit" (Jeremiah 17: 8).

The world tells us to reach for everything else but Jesus. Sadly, most people do until they're faced with a tragedy or trauma and the only thing left to do is pray. God sometimes uses events like these to bring us closer to Him. Afterall, that's all He wants from us. He's desperate for our attention, and nowadays, He is competing against a lot more things than He used to have to. The world runs at such a fast-pace, we never stop doing. The summer flies by, all of a sudden school starts, then it's Halloween. Before you know it, you start Christmas shopping, you celebrate the new year, you count down the days until spring and the next thing you know, it's summer again.

Success

I first fell in love with success in 2010 after getting fired as a telemarketer and interviewing at a marketing firm. During the interview, I was basically told that the only reason why I was getting this job at the firm was because I had experience talking on the phone 40 hours a week and that's what it took to be great at recruiting for their company. Gosh, I hated that telemarketing job and being on the phone for 40 hours, but I took the job at the firm anyway because of the compensation, hours, and opportunity for advancement. I got to travel all over the country and stay in penthouse suites, hang out with a bunch of rich people, and eat and drink off the company's dime. We attended massive seminars and conventions where tens of thousands of people would watch the top people get called up on stage and be awarded checks, gifts, and rings for their hard work. They would give a motivational speech about how anyone can get to the top with hard work, dedication, and sacrifice and if you do things now that nobody else wants to do, then you'll have things later that nobody else will have. And although that quote sounds good in theory and I'm even guilty of posting it on social media back in my hustle days, why does it matter if you have things other people don't? And what if there never is a "later"? "Later" never came for my uncle after he lost his battle with cancer before his 50th birthday. He and my aunt had all these plans of what they would do after their seven kids grew up and moved out. They were going to travel, spend time together, do ministry work, raise up grandchildren and so much more, but he never got to because his time to enter Heaven had come when we least expected it to. James 4:14 says, "Yet you do not know what tomorrow will bring. What is your life? For you are a mist that appears for a little time and then vanishes."

After the session was over, the speakers and top salesmen and saleswomen would stand outside the doors and would have lines of people waiting to take their picture and talk to them. I saw how people looked at them, how they adored them, and praised them. I didn't know how it would happen but I was willing to sacrifice anything to achieve it.

"Thus says the Lord: 'Cursed is the man who trusts in man and makes flesh his strength, whose heart turns away from the Lord. He is like a shrub in the desert, and shall not see any good come. He shall dwell in the parched places of the wilderness, in an uninhabited salt land'" (Jeremiah 17:5).

I began working as hard as I could to get a promotion, and within a year, I got one. I was the head recruiter in my office, the boss's right-hand person. This was a huge win for me, or so I thought, because it meant more money and more authority, but it also meant more responsibility and now more sacrifice. I was expected to work longer hours, achieve higher recruiting goals if I wanted to get to that next level because now I was "competing" against people at a higher caliber who wanted this success as badly as I did. My hard work paid off and I was promoted again, this time becoming the head of the entire department, in charge of nine offices and their recruiting departments. I was required to travel to different offices on weekends, going days without seeing my 2-year-old twin boys and living a life where I wouldn't see them for more than an hour at night and an hour in the morning before dropping them off at daycare. I was sacrificing everything that was important for worldly success because I needed validation.

I kept this up for another three years before I cracked. About once a month I would stand outside the building on my lunch break, chain smoking cigarettes and crying to my husband John on the phone. I would tell him how stressed I was, how I couldn't keep going, and I just felt so out of alignment with my life, but we needed the money and knew my "big break" had to be coming just around the corner, so I held on a little longer. So for a total of five years, I talked myself into keeping this job, even though I knew from the interview that the job wasn't for me, but I knew I would one day finally get the approval I had longed for. I missed the first five years of my twins' lives.

After getting pregnant with our daughter, I really began hating long hours, traveling, and sacrifice. And with the help of my raging hormones, I couldn't stand anyone and everything and began to loathe this job, but I stayed. Why? Mostly fear, self-doubt, comparison, and idolizing success. I was now chained to this career because without the praise, recognition, and success, I was a nobody (or so I thought). I needed their praises to fill my tank, but once it was full, it was empty the next day. Not only was my mental health deteriorating, but my physical health was also taking a toll on my body now being pregnant and being on the road more days than I wasn't. I was diagnosed with two different autoimmune diseases.

My mom was very big into natural health, she cured herself (with God's help of course) of ovarian cancer when I was in 11th grade, and ever since then, she made it her full-time job researching supplements and natural cures to America's common diseases. She partnered with a health and wellness direct sales company, begged me to join her team, and connected me to other moms who had the freedom to work when and where they wanted and were making six and seven-figure incomes. So, one day when our daughter was about six months old, I walked into work and just cracked. I couldn't do it one more day and I quit on the spot, packed up my office and drove home.

It's so cool when you're able to look back and see how God prepared you at every stage in life with your future in mind. The telemarketing job gave me the skills I needed to recruit for the firm. The recruiting, leadership, and sales skills I learned at the firm set me up for success in the direct sales world. God will never waste your time; He uses every experience to prepare you for what's to come.

Within three years, I became a top-earner in my new company and was making multiple 6-figures per year, thinking I had finally arrived and all of my hard work was paying off. But, I quickly ran into the same problem as before. More money came from more people being successful on my team, which gave me more responsibility and more people to depend on me. I was spread thinner than ever, my mental health was dwindling, and every breath I took was a struggle and now was pregnant with baby number four.

See, I thought what I was after was money, success, status, and wealth since that filled the void (temporarily) in my life. But what I was really after was freedom, fulfillment, alignment, and purpose. My depression, anxiety, and stress built up for three more years before I was able to let go of the idol, quit the industry for good, and move forward after having the encounter with God in my bathroom.

Change

So, how long are you going to swap out one coping mechanism for the next? How long are you going to sit inside of the Valley totally miserable waiting for things to change but doing the exact same thing every day? After all, the definition of insanity given by the brilliant Albert Einstein is "Doing the same thing over and over again but expecting a different result."

I recommend adding this prayer to your daily routine: "Lord, light the path for my future and slam the door on paths that don't serve me." God knows you better than you know yourself, and He knows how stubborn and fearful you can be.

Write down at the top of your journal pages "Prayers" and then write my prayer above on the first line so you don't forget it.

I am incredibly grateful for every opportunity that God has given me (even if I felt miserable in the moment) because everyone I met, everything I saw, and every experience I had, molded me into who I am today. In hindsight, I can see how God used all things in my life for His glory and goodness.

Preparation

A few months ago, I watched a documentary on Netflix called "14 Peaks" about this man who wanted more than anything to hike the 14 mountains in the world that are higher than 8,000 meters in just seven months. Everyone told him that it was impossible, nobody else had done it before, or even came close. The fastest time recorded up until this date was seven years. Yes, I said years... and he wanted to do it in just seven months. But he was ready. He trained, he prayed, he consulted with experts, he believed he could do it, he surrounded himself with people who supported him and lifted him up with encouragement and guided him every step of the way. Go watch the trailer on Youtube and listen to the words.

Whether you're hiking the 14 peaks or your own personal peaks and valleys, it's going to require you to train the same. You're going to need a team of people to help you achieve this, and that is why I am showing up for you as your own personal hiking guide. I have been where you are, I know what it takes to get out and rise above. I can recognize the warning signs that you're about to fall into a pit, and I can tell you what to do when things start to go wrong. I know what you will have to endure ahead, and it is my job to point you to God and the resources that will take you further than you ever imagined.

If you're like me, when I started this journey, you probably don't have a lot of people surrounding you, encouraging you, pouring God's truth into you, loving you unconditionally, cheering for your healing and walking with you every step of the way with no judgment but only love.

The world is a dark place. Remember, most people are broken themselves, just trying to survive, coping with anything that makes them feel better in the moment, allowing their emotions to sway them with the wind. If you've experienced trauma, abuse, or you struggle with mental health like I do, there's not many people willing to open up and relate to you and empathize with your struggle, and that's hard. That is why I created a podcast to link like-minded women together who are desperately trying to live for Jesus in a world filled with darkness. My podcast can be found anywhere you listen to podcasts and is called "WAKE UP! With Tarryn Sarcone." This platform is used to teach what I am learning and going through in real time. I get raw and real while I learn my own triggers, my own wounds, recognize my own sin and scars that are holding me back from an intimate relationship with Jesus.

If you want to connect with me deeper after reading this book, please start your day out by waking up with me and listening to any episode that connects with your spirit.

Write down another prayer in your journal for the perfect connections to be made so that you can plug into God's community of people and find your soul sisters. The Bible is filled with scriptures pointing us to community with other Christians, and I've learned first-hand how important it is for protection against the enemy. We teach our kids that there is "strength in numbers," so it's about time we begin believing that for ourselves. When I started praying for connections and for God to bring me my people, He immediately answered my prayers and started connecting me to so many women who I felt I have known forever. God has used them to encourage, protect, speak life over me, and guide me. This book wouldn't be written without them, my podcast wouldn't exist, and I would bet that I would be stuck down in a pit somewhere sulking, crying, and wondering what to do next.

For the complete list of prayers I say on a daily basis that you can use, visit www.tarrynsarcone.com/thevalley

Now, don't start idolizing people and relationships, because we need to keep our eyes on Jesus, and we really don't need anything else besides Him. But remember, God knows our personalities. He knows who we are on the deepest, most intimate level, so He knows that we need people on our path to validate, encourage, and point us in the right direction. Fear can be very overwhelming and is one of the top things that holds us back from moving forward—fear of the unknown, fear of failure, fear of what others might think, so it's important to have a group of women in our corner encouraging us to move forward. Community is crucial in your journey out of the Valley.

"Two are better than one, because they have a good reward for their toil. For if they fall, one will lift up his fellow. But woe to him who is alone when he falls and has not another to lift him up! Again, if two lie together, they keep warm, but how can one keep warm alone? And though a man might prevail against one who is alone, two will withstand him—a threefold cord is not quickly broken" (Ecclesiastes 4:9-12 [ESV]).

TURN ON THE LIGHTS

When I was about five years old, I started totally freaking everyone out around me by sleepwalking in the middle of the night. One time when I was in middle school, I was woken up by my aunt as I tried escaping the second story balcony of my grandma's cabin by climbing over the railing. I would try walking out of hotel rooms while on vacation and would even find myself turned around in my own bedroom, not knowing which way to go to get to the hallway so that I could find the bathroom in a room that was pitch black.

Our brains play funny tricks on us, especially when we can't see anything, when we're focused on something completely different and don't know which way to go.

This is the exact same thing that is happening to you right now in the Valley. Your brain is playing tricks on you and it's time we wake up, turn the lights on, and expose the devil and his schemes. You were not created to live in this turmoil, this stress, this day-to-day hell of misery, mental illness, and feelings of being crazy. In the next chapter, we're really going to spend some time together getting into your identity and how God created you to live. But first, we need to expose the devil so he no longer has power over your life. If he can distract you by getting you to focus on something else, he wins. It's as simple as that. He doesn't need to totally destroy your family, attack you from every angle, and ruin every good thing that's ever come to you, like he did with Job in order to take you down.

Awareness

What I've found to be true with my own life and the thousands of women I've coached is that all he needs to do is get us to focus on anything else besides God and His word. When I was younger, he got me to focus on popularity and fitting in. When I became an adult, he got me to focus on success and money. What are you focusing on? Is it a goal? Or is it fear and worry? Or maybe you've lived a life where all you were able to focus on was surviving? Write down at the top of a fresh page in your journal: "What consumes my mind most of my days?" and take some time to pray first that God reveals your truth to you and then start writing whatever comes to your mind without trying to make sense of it.

Whenever we're in a Valley, our minds are racing with negative, stressful things so whatever is consuming your mind, what does the Bible have to say about that? My favorite website to visit is www.gotquestions.org and there you can ask any question you have regarding God. If it's anxiety, fear or worry, type in to that site, "What does the Bible say about anxiety?" or "What does the Bible say about fear?" and do some reading and research for yourself.

As you're discovering God's advice in the scriptures on these topics, pull out your favorite scriptures and write them on notecards and tape them up around your house.

Here's my favorite scripture I've found on anxiety that is actually written with a wet-erase marker on my bathroom mirror:

"Do not be anxious about anything, but in everything by prayer and supplication with thanksgiving let your requests be made known to God. And the peace of God, which surpasses all understanding, will guard your hearts and your minds in Christ Jesus" (Philippians 4:6-7 [ESV]).

I recommend writing the scriptures down somewhere that you can see them daily and recite them out loud when you do. Studies show that if you do this, you will be 10x more likely to live out the scriptures because now you're writing it down, reading it out loud, and then hearing yourself read it. This is extremely powerful and I have done this religiously the last five years of my life.

The most important thing you can do right now is identify and name the thing that's consuming you. It might be financial stress, relationship struggles, your future, your kids, health, or even an addiction you are trying to let go of and manage. Maybe it's ten different things that are adding up.

In Sarah Young's Devotional *Jesus Calling*, she writes, "Your deepest most constant need is for My Peace. I have planted Peace in the garden of your heart, where I live, but there are weeds growing there too: pride, worry, selfishness, unbelief. I am the Gardener, and I am working to rid your heart of those weeds. I do My work in various ways. When you sit quietly with Me, I shine the Light of My Presence directly into your heart. In this heavenly Light, Peace grows abundantly and weeds shrivel up. I also send trials into your life. When you trust Me in the midst of trouble, Peace flourishes and weeds die away. Thank Me for troublesome situations; the Peace they can produce *far outweighs* the trials you endure" (based on Philippians 4:19; 2 Corinthians 4:17 [ESV]).

Whatever it is that you're struggling with, you need to spend time with God for Him to shine His Light on those areas of your heart.

Think of the value of a lamp in a dark place. The light it brings, the goodness, the direction, the comfort and security. Now think of what the lamp provides in a dark room with no electricity. Nothing. Without the source, the lamp is useless, so when we get you plugged into the source and walking in the light, that's when the real magic happens.

God's Will

One way we can live in the light is by focusing and living in the present. The devil will try to distract you from doing this and pull you back into the darkness by bringing up your past to dwell on or allow your mind to race with fears, worries, and goals of tomorrow. But what is happening today that you're ignoring?

To live completely in God's will and light today, it will require you to be present, plugged into the source in order to be in a good mood (more on this later), and to take good care of things God has already blessed you with. This includes being available to those around you who need you. If you're focused on tomorrow, you're not able to be in God's will today, so I've found your mindset is one of the most important things, if not the most important thing to have in check in order to get out and stay out of the Valley. If you struggle with being present, I recommend you read the book *Present Over Perfect* by Shauna Niequist. This book was life-changing for me when I was first learning this.

You're going to hear me give tons of tools and resources in this book, some of them you may not feel like you need, while other things instantly connect with your spirit. This is how you're going to learn to operate your life with God and allow the Spirit to lead and guide you. He makes certain things known because it's what He wants you to do next while other things go in one ear and out the other.

When it comes to living in the light and being in God's will today, it's going to require you to be a good steward of what He has already blessed you with. So, what is the current status of your home? Is it neat, organized, and clean? What about your car? Are you praying for God to bless you with more—more money, more success, or more kids? All while drowning in what you currently have? Our Father knows what we need more than we know what we need and if you can't tithe 10% consistently now out of $100, I highly doubt you'll be able to give back to the kingdom when you have $1,000 or $10,000. If you can't manage your money well now when you barely have any, how do you think you'll do if He opens the floodgates and blesses you abundantly? Are you losing it on your kids and blowing up with rage and anger but then praying He gives you more? God will not give us more until we show Him how we can handle what we already have. So being a good steward of the things today will equal more blessings tomorrow.

Studies show that when you are disorganized and living around clutter that you get overwhelmed easier, your mental health is worse off than someone living in organization and order. I call these energy leaks and we have an entire chapter dedicated to learning about what's causing your energy to leak out of your life and walk in darkness again.

Start a new page in your journal and write at the top: "I am grateful for..."? Setting your mind on gratitude is a great way to walk in the light by shifting your perspective from a half empty glass to a half full glass. If you prefer, you can pick up a gratitude journal on Amazon or any book store if it will help you to stay organized.

Bottom line, you need to spend some time figuring out what is keeping you in darkness and away from the source of light. Call it out by writing it down, finding scriptures that speak the truth on the topic, and by praying God helps you to stay plugged in.

"Blessed are those who have learned to walk in the light of your presence" (Psalm 89:15).

CHOSEN

In 2022, my husband and I traveled to Nashville, Tennessee and had the opportunity to take a backstage tour of the Grand Ole' Opry. I've always been a lover of all music, so when I heard the story behind the Opry, I was blown away. There we learned about all the artists who strived to earn an invitation to play at the Opry, but also about those who longed for the exclusive invitation to become an official member of the Grand Ole' Opry. We heard story after story about artists who grew up knowing that one day they would perform there. They didn't know how or when, but they had a deep-down belief that it was more than just a dream.

I couldn't help but think of all of the people who should be performing there but aren't and it's not because of their skill level. It's their disbelief, their skewed perception of themselves. The reason why most people never make it on stage at the Opry or the stage of life is because they don't believe that they can—they don't believe they're special or chosen to do great things.

Over the years, I've learned that you don't have to be the best at something in order to start doing it. The only thing you need is to believe in yourself enough to get started and then keep going. The world's best artist isn't the most skilled artist in the world—they're simply the person who believed they could create and then started doing it. Meanwhile, someone out there could have way better skills but if they never believe they can do it, they never will. It's the same in any industry. Fear of not being good enough or failing.

What has been on your heart and mind to do for a while but you haven't started? Take a minute and sit with God asking Him that question. I even recommend writing down what you hear so that you don't ever forget it.

It's time we start listening to God and following His direction in order to accomplish the things in life we know we were set out to do. In order to do this, we have to understand who God says we are because our definitions of ourselves aren't going to cut it.

After hearing God speak to me in my bathroom and tell me that I was Chosen & Anointed to do big things, I decided right then and there that I was going to tap into exactly who God made me to be and figure out my purpose here on earth once and for all.

In order to do that, I had to start with His words.

The following chapters outline exactly what I did to get myself out of the Valley with God's help and onto the highest peak of the tallest mountain and now I'm here sharing it with you.

Believe

The first thing you need to do is BELIEVE in who God says you are, you can't just know it, you have to believe it. The Bible is extremely clear on our identity in Christ, why He created us, how He created us to be, and our purpose here on earth, but I found two big reasons why we don't take God at His word.

The first one is that we don't know His word. The second is that we've believed what others have said we were instead of Christ, our Creator.

Here's what The Creator says about you:

You are a Daughter of the Highest King, you have peace with God, the Holy Spirit lives in you, you are no longer condemned, you are completely forgiven, tenderly loved, and the light of the world.

You are firmly rooted and built up in Christ, born of God and the evil one cannot touch you. You may approach God with boldness, freedom, and confidence. You have been rescued from Satan's domain and transferred into the kingdom of Christ forever. You have been given a spirit of power, love, and self-discipline, all your needs are met by God, and all things are currently working together in your life for the goodness of God.

Nothing you can do will ever separate you from the love of God, no sin, no evil, no thought, or desire. You cannot be separated from God. You are his workmanship, and you can do all things through Christ who gives you the strength you need in every moment.

Why is it that we can believe in God's word and believe it to be true in anyone else's life except our own. It's easy for us to see the greatness in others, but when it comes to looking in the mirror, we only see the ugly, the bad, and the broken. Reading those scriptures about yourself I imagine was difficult to really believe deep down in your soul and that's okay. It took me a solid year of reciting them to believe them.

One in eight Christians say that they read their Bible regularly. So, if the other seven of us don't ever read the manual to life, the handbook to how we're supposed to live, then how in the world would we know how to do it?

It's like buying a bike online that's delivered in a box in pieces and never reading the instructions. You struggle to put it together, thinking you'll win some kind of badge of honor for doing it alone without the help of the creator of the bike. Why do we do this? Why do we think if we can get through life on our own, we're stronger people? We could avoid so much frustration, stress and turmoil if we just read the instructions first. Instead, we get mad at the bike, it's never rideable, and your child falls to the ground in a full-out meltdown.

Why do we get angry at how our life is going if we never bother to read the manual? And I'm just as guilty of this as you. I've considered myself a Christian for a very long time and can say, up until this ah-ha moment, I had never opened my Bible and read it for clarity or direction in my life. It just sat on my bookshelf.

So why don't we read it?

I think this is where we need to start in order to get you reading it daily. The first reason I hear is that we don't understand the Bible and how it is written. The Bible says that we won't understand it until we have the Holy Spirit in us to interpret what it's saying. So, like I said in the previous chapter, start by asking the Holy Spirit to dwell within you. Tell God you know that His Son was sent here on earth to die on the cross as a sacrifice for your sins. Tell Him you are ready to surrender your life and live a life of wholeness and purpose and purity with His help. Pray that the Holy Spirit enters your soul and begins to change you to be more like God. I promise, if you truly believe what you're saying, and pray with bold audacity then you will be saved by eternal sufferings and the Holy Spirit will begin to speak to you and guide you. You need the Spirit's help. You can't do this your way any longer.

"Everything is possible for the one who believes" (Mark 9:32).

The Handbook

You also need to get yourself a Bible that is written in a style or vernacular that you understand, and purchasing a Bible written in plain English just simply isn't going to be enough. The English language has changed so much since the days of cavemen to Shakespeare to now, if you tried to read an old Shakespear book, it would probably be hard for you to understand it.

The versions of the Bible that I can most easily understand are NLT (New Living Translation), NIV (New International Version), or ESV (English Standard Version).

You're going to come across words while you're reading that you don't understand, so what I do is look up the definition of the word and then circle the word in my Bible and draw an arrow over to the side where I write a different word for that word so I can understand better. The goal when reading your Bible isn't to fly through it and read it as fast as you can like a fictional chapter book. It's more like a study, a slow-roll read through it, looking to fully understand each sentence that connects to your soul. As you read, especially if you pray before you begin reading, you will connect certain things you read to your current life struggles, desires, and needs. This is your spirit connecting with the Holy Spirit and helping you to understand, exactly as the scripture describes.

"All Scripture is God-breathed and is useful for teaching, rebuking, correcting and training in righteousness..." 2 Timothy 3:16

The next excuse I hear people making about reading their Bible is that they don't know where to start, and this was my excuse forever. So, I bought myself a chronological Bible which means they took all the events that are mentioned in the Bible and they put them in order from first to last. This helps you to open the book at the beginning and read it from front to back like a story.

It's split into two parts, first It's the history of the world, starting at its creation, then we learn about the people who heard from God, obeyed His commands and changed the world as we know it. This first part is called The Old Testament. Then it goes into the New Testament, talking about all the miracles and wonders Jesus performed while He was living on earth as a human, instructions to His disciples and the people who would gather to hear His sermons. It describes the fight Jesus gave for you and I in the tragic love story of His crucifixion. The Bible then ends with the book of Revelation describing end-times when Jesus returns on a white horse and saves us all from this evil, sinful world we live in and conquers darkness for good. Hallelujah!

You can go to www.tarrynsarcone.com/thevalley and purchase the exact Bible I use that I bought from Amazon for less than $20. Start by challenging yourself to read 15 minutes every day, whether it's first when you wake up, in the middle of the day or before you go to bed, but see if you can do it for seven days in a row.

(Pro tip: Sometimes the people's names in the Bible can be hard to pronounce and understand, especially in the beginning of the Bible in Genesis as you read the family trees and the genealogy. Don't let this discourage you. This list is good if you're going back to study a specific family, but I skip past those parts to allow me to keep focused and understand what I'm reading.)

If you really want to make a difference in the way you see yourself and the influence you have, then I highly recommend going to www.tarrynsarcone.com/thevalley and downloading your free copy of your "Identity & Inheritance" to print out and read out loud every single day. This is the list of scriptures I just gave you but written in first person. Tape this to your wall or your fridge. The devil cannot read your mind, so once he hears you read this list out loud, he will know that you know the truth and you are ready for war. And the best news is that we've already won it.

Rebellion

The devil has been after you in a non-stop tug-of-war battle since before you were born. His goal is to trick you, deceive you, and lie to you, just like he did to the first humans created on earth, Adam and Eve. Satan immediately tempted the couple to doubt God's goodness and despite God calling them "image bearers in God's likeness" when He created them, they still were deceived by Satan! He tricked them to believe that God wasn't good and that rebellion would give them greater identities. The apple doesn't fall far from the tree.

Second Corinthians 11:3 ESV says, "But I am afraid that as the serpent deceived Eve by his cunning, your thoughts will be led astray from a sincere and pure devotion to Christ."

It's extremely important that you understand that your natural draw to rebellion is because it was inherited to you. There is nothing wrong with you. In fact, it would be impossible for you to not have rebellion in you and for you to want to live a wholesome, pure life and not do things to sabotage that like sinning. Everyone sins. Everyone has rebellion. We all reject authority and exchange good for evil. *Romans 3:23 states, "For we have all sinned and fall short of the glory of God."* It is human nature to reject God's voice. It's natural to embrace identities different from who God made us to be.

We rebel, live in pain, and die. God's way has become unnatural to us. Humans are by nature separated from God, the eternal source of life. Death (separation) is our eternal condition. But Jesus, the eternal Son of God, became human to reclaim you from death. His death offers you a way to re-identify with God and freedom from rebellion. Accepting Christ as your savior gives you a new nature (the Spirit), and eternal life.

New Identity

The Father has reclaimed and chosen us, through his Son; Jesus as His children. He did this because of His love for us. He wants us to know Him for who He is and reflect His image. We are being restored right now for the purpose God intended for all of mankind before Adam and Eve's sinful fall. If you fully trust Jesus to save you from sin and say the prayer mentioned previously, then God will give you a brand-new identity.

How sad would it be for someone created for so much amazing-ness, who inherited all of those things above to simply not access any of it because they didn't believe they were chosen? Don't let this be the story of your life. You must believe you are chosen for something more—for greatness. Once you fully believe that with all of your heart, you will loosen the chains the devil has around you and you will be able to begin your journey into the full and abundant life God intended for you.

Ephesians 2:1-6 that says: "Once you were dead because of your disobedience and your many sins. You used to live in sin, just like the rest of the world, obeying the devil—the commander of the powers in the unseen world. He is the spirit at work in the hearts of those who refuse to obey God. All of us used to live that way, following the passionate desires and inclinations of our sinful nature. By our very nature we were subject to God's anger, just like everyone else. But God is so rich in mercy, and he loved us so much that even though we were dead because of our sins, he gave us life when he raised Christ from the dead. (It is only by God's grace that you have been saved!) For he raised us from the dead along with Christ and seated us with him in the heavenly realms because we are united with Christ Jesus."

ANOINTED

My entire life, I believed that if I wanted something bad enough, I could work hard, sacrifice, and get it. But I eventually realized this was not true in every situation. I wanted success in my network marketing business more than I wanted to breathe, and I was sacrificing everything to get it. I was holding onto the hope that eventually it will come. The money did, but the success didn't. Success isn't defined by how much money you have or a specific rank or achievement—it's based on a feeling. There are plenty of millionaires out there who do not feel successful. We want to *feel* successful which is really hard since a feeling is based on an emotion, and emotions are constantly changing. We will be diving deeper into emotional lenses later on in this book, but for now, **I want you to realize that you are not in complete control over the success in your life if God isn't on board with your plans.** If God doesn't want you to do something, you won't ever be able to be successful at doing it. It's as simple as that.

God has given you specific skills, talents, and gifts that He wanted you to be able to use to further His mission here on earth, which is spreading the good news and living a life modeled after Christ. And although you are so talented, special, and unique... you can probably think of some talents and skills God didn't give you. Maybe you absolutely love to sing like me. Music is in your soul, but when it comes to having the skill of singing, you may lack it a little...or a lot. No matter how hard I try, no matter how many singing lessons I pay for or stages I attempt to perform on... I will never sound like Mariah Carey, and it's just the facts. I wasn't born with the ability to sing, and that's okay because what I was born with is just as incredible as Mariah Carey's gifts. I was born with unique gifts, and so were you. *1 Corinthians 12: 4-6 reads, "Now there are varieties of gifts, but the same Spirit; and there are varieties of service, but the same Lord; and there are varieties of activities, but it is the same God who empowers them all in everyone."*

For too long, I compared myself to others, believed in what they said about me, and tried to desperately fit in and belong where I simply didn't. I needed people to approve of me in order to feel like I mattered, but I had it all wrong.

After finally believing in who God said I was, something inside of me changed. The feeling of success that I had been after my entire life was present, and this time it wasn't based on a dollar amount in my bank account or a certain level of achievement at work. It was a feeling of fulfillment, confidence, joy and gratitude that would never be taken away again because it wasn't based on circumstances. It was based on connecting to my Creator and believing in who He created me to be.

I saw it. My own uniqueness, my own skills and talents God had placed in me. I no longer hated myself or was embarrassed by my personality, shrinking myself to fit in other people's boxes. Instead, I found myself bolder, more confident, and people would tell me on a regular basis I looked like I was glowing. You can tell when someone is truly happy and aligned with their purpose or if they're just faking it. Especially after you yourself have walked through this transition, you can spot a lost soul from a mile away.

Chances are, this lost soul is still you right now, and all I want you to do is to be aware.

Awareness is the second thing you need to do after believing in who you are. It's being aware of where you're truly at in your life and it's the beautiful moment when you surrender it all to God. You wave your white flag in defeat and admit you have no clue what you're doing. He will only take over control of the ship if we take our hands off the wheel, and until we do that, He will stand next to us, waiting patiently. He is a perfect gentleman who operates in love. Love is not forceful or demanding. Love is patient and love is kind, so He will patiently wait for you to make this decision and give him the wheel.

Beauty in the Breakdown

So, have you asked Him to take control? If you haven't had that moment with God, stop this book and take a minute to ask God to take control of your life. Let Him know how defeated and exhausted you are and how badly you need Him. Admit you can't do this alone anymore and you're ready to let go of the control and follow His lead over your life. Don't miss this step; it's extremely important.

Now, it may not feel so beautiful while you're face down on your bathroom floor with mascara running down your cheeks, you're hyperventilating, the kids screaming at the door to come in, and everything that could go wrong has gone wrong. In fact, it probably feels the exact opposite of beautiful, but I promise you that once you're out of this emotion, you're going to look back and view it as one of your most beautiful moments in your life. I wish someone would have told me at that moment that it gets better.

I promise you—God can be trusted and if you follow this book and do what I did. I promise you with everything I have that it will get better for you too. God promises to help us if we call out. He promises and he has never once ever broken a promise. *"He will call upon Me, and I will answer him; I will be with him in trouble; I will rescue him and honor him" (Psalm 91:15).*

Once you can admit that your life isn't going the way you had imagined it to go, God can begin to put it back together in the way He intended it to be the whole time and that path He has chosen for you is anointed.

Following

Because we are used to controlling our lives, our plans, and futures, we tend to spend a lot of our time plotting, planning, and scheming our way to the top. The second you realize you're enough, you always have been and you're ready to step into what that looks like, your brain will immediately start thinking of all the ways you can use your newfound skills and talents. Don't get overwhelmed, and don't get ahead of God. Remember, you are no longer in control, and the future is really none of your business. Your job is to spend as much time abiding in God as you can. You can do this by reading His word and praying, which will allow you to hear the ideas and direction He gives you through the Holy Spirit or the things He puts directly on your path (more on this later.)

The important thing to remember is that He has anointed you to do this. *1 John 2:27 says, "But the anointing that you received from him abides in you, and you have no need that anyone should teach you.*

But as his anointing teaches you about everything, and is true, and is no lie—just as it has taught you, abide in him."

Learning to be still and quiet in order to hear from God will take some time to learn at first. Start out by thinking of something you really want to accomplish—maybe it's to feel better, maybe it's a company you're starting or a brand you've always wanted to launch. Maybe it's a book you want to write, a podcast to record, a relationship to restore, or a ministry to join. Whatever the thing is that you want to move forward, stop and think for a few minutes and ask God what is the next thing you should do in order to move you in the right direction? I only want you to think about the very next thing you should do. Don't think about what it will take to do it or anything else.

An example of this is if you want to start feeling better, think of the very first thing you need to do. Do you need to stop drinking alcohol or smoking weed? Do you need to start reading your Bible daily? Do you need to start moving your body or eating better? I'm sure it's all of the above, but what is the one thing God is telling you to start or stop? Stop this book and write down it down in your journal so you don't forget.

Chances are you don't even need a few minutes to do this. You could probably think of the next thing you need to do immediately which proves you do know what to do and you do have the ability to listen to your intuition, AKA the Holy Spirit guiding you, so stop saying you don't know what to do.

But almost immediately after thinking of the next thing you need to do, fear probably pops up and starts saying, "I don't know how to do that." "Will that really work?" "What if I fail?" "What if I can't stop?" "What if they reject me?" "What if I look stupid?" "I'm scared to do that." "I'm not good enough."

...And the list goes on and on.

But remember, it's not just you doing this alone anymore. You are anointed! The definition of anointed is: chosen by or as if by divine authority; chosen for a sacred, high, or special vocation or purpose.

You're not in charge of making sure you are equipped enough to tackle your purpose. Do you know that God actually doesn't want us to be equipped and ready, because when that happens, we no longer need to rely on Him? He wants us to rely on Him entirely and He wants all the glory.

When God chose Moses to go talk to the leaders in Israel and demand the Pharoah to let God's people go, He didn't first look at who was the best presenter and persuader who spoke the clearest in order to fulfill His plan. Instead, God looked at who would answer the call, who was paying attention, and who would be willing to trust God to perform a miracle through him. God spoke to Moses through a burning bush that caught his attention. I would say that if a bush was burning today, most of us would be too distracted to even notice, our faces focused so intently on a screen in our hand.

God doesn't call the already equipped—He equips the ones who answer the calling.

The Bible mentions that Moses wasn't a good speaker, and some scholars say he had some sort of speech impediment that caused him to not communicate well, but God still chose Him and then anointed him to be able to do it. This is only one story from the Bible. Most of the people that are recorded in the Bible for doing amazing things weren't equipped at all to do them. In fact, most people made fun of them, told them they couldn't do it, or mocked them. But they knew their God would not let them fail, they knew they were called to do something and because they believed in who they were, and heard what they were called to do, they trusted in God to fulfill His mission through them and anoint them for greatness.

Mary was a virgin who was told by an angel at age 14 she was pregnant with the Messiah.

Noah was told to build an arc for a great flood coming when it hadn't rained in over 40 years.

Jonah was told to deliver a powerful message to a sinful, violent city called Nineveh to repent and turn from their evil ways.

Gideon was from the lowest family and was called to destroy Israel's enemies.

David was only a child who believed he could defeat Goliath and then did.

Mary Magdalene was possessed by seven demons and healed by Jesus proving that no demons or evil spirits can withstand the presence of God.

Rahab was a prostitute in Jericho that God used to take down the city and deliver it into the hands of God's chosen people.

You are no different than Moses, Mary, Jonah or any other character we learn about from the Bible. God has a huge plan for your life and wants to use you in ways you could never even begin to imagine. But, in order to do this, you have to believe who your creator says you are.

Once you start to spend time with him—talking, listening, and learning, you will start to understand more about your purpose and anointing. God leads you down your path of destiny one step at a time leaving a trail of breadcrumbs to follow.

Answer the Call

The saddest part to me is that so many women never hear God calling them because they're too busy, too distracted, and everything is just too loud. There are so many women who have been called, and it's not that they don't answer the call because they're fearful, but because they don't even hear the phone ringing.

Jesus is calling you... Have you heard Him? Do you feel this pull in you to do something more, something greater? Have you had encounters with Him? Weird "coincidental" things that happen, like maybe even finding this book at the perfect time in the most random way? How long has He been calling you and you've been ignoring Him or you just flat out didn't hear? For me it was years, probably 20 or more, that I ignored His call. I wonder how much further ahead I could be in my walk with Him on my life's mission if I would've listened way back then (and how much pain I could've avoided).

Unfortunately, we can't go back in time, but what matters is what we do now. I want to help you realize that He is not expecting you to say yes and do it alone. He knows you don't feel worthy. He knows you don't feel ready or good enough. He knows you aren't equipped to do the thing that He has laid in your heart, but with Him, through Him, He will equip you more than you could ever imagine. All He needs is for you to be willing to go and rely on Him for the rest.

You have everything you already need because of the anointing through the Holy Spirit in your life and if you don't feel this or believe it yet, ask God to reveal it to you. He will teach you everything you need to know. Don't let the phone keep on ringing while you're self-medicating, numbing, and distracting yourself. You can do this because of Him. It's time to pick up the phone and hear the mission God has for your life. You are equipped and anointed because of Him.

CHAPTER 4

"Now may the God of peace who brought again from the dead our Lord Jesus, the great shepherd of the sheep, by the blood of the eternal covenant, equip you with everything good that you may do his will, working in us that which is pleasing in his sight, through Jesus Christ, to whom be glory forever and ever. Amen" (Hebrews 13:20-21 [ESV]).

CHAPTER 5

ATTACKED AT CONCEPTION

In December of 1988, my mom was 19 years old and desperately wanted to fit in and be approved of in the world. So, instead of seeking her identity and worth through her creator, she sought after the approval and comfort of man, believing who they said she was, wanting desperately to feel important, special, and unique. She found herself pregnant and in a broken relationship, causing even more damage. She ended up giving birth to me shortly after her 20th birthday and did the very best she could with what she had. Up until last year when I "intuitively" knew I needed to go seek professional counseling (don't worry, the counseling chapter is coming, I promise!), I blamed her for a lot of my trauma, hardships, and generational sins she passed down to me.

Now I say, "She did the best she could with what she had" because that was her heart. She is a phenomenal mother, always thinking and putting her children first. She would do anything to protect us and raise us the right way, giving us everything we needed and never letting a day pass without telling us how much she loved and adored us. And I'm sure, if you're a mother, you would say you feel the same way. In your heart, you love those kids more than life itself, you would do anything for them, but because we are broken ourselves, and because this world is broken, and because we are not perfect like Jesus, we make mistakes and we're triggered often by our past. We lash out in anger at our children and explode with rage to only feel an immense amount of guilt and shame afterwards that leads you basically crawling into their rooms begging for forgiveness. We say things we don't mean, we make choices that we know are poor, and we cope with things of this world way more than we would be willing to admit we do. We're not perfect parents, but deep down, we love those kids, and therefore we do the very best we can with what we have. For some moms, that's not very much at all, but it's all they have.

Influence

When you look at generational trauma and sin, abuse, neglect, and abandonment, what you'll see is that the more messed up someone is, chances are their parents were even more messed up. Now obviously this isn't true for every situation, but for most of them that is what researchers have found. If you grew up in an abusive home, chances are you'll find yourself in the same situation again, either by doing the abusing or by you being a victim of the abuse as an adult. Fifty-one percent of adults found themselves in abusive situations again after escaping abuse as a child. Because it's how you were raised, it's what was normal to you, and how you saw emotions modeled, you learned from watching your surroundings, that is the way to act.

Even if you knew that these things were bad, you found yourself "fitting in" at times with your family in a bad way doing and becoming the things you've always hated and resented because of your immediate circle of influence. You become who you surround yourself with whether you like it or not. Our brains mock and imitate things that we see and hear over time, that is why you need to be extremely careful to guard what you see and hear, but don't worry, we also have a whole chapter dedicated to this toward the end of the book.

Have you ever heard the fable of the Eagle and the Chicken? It's about an eagle that thought he was a chicken. When the eagle was very small, he fell from the safety of his nest. A chicken farmer found the eagle, brought him to the farm, and raised him in a chicken coop among his many chickens. The eagle grew up doing what chickens do, living like a chicken, and believing he was a chicken.

A naturalist came to the chicken farm to see if what he had heard about an eagle acting like a chicken was really true. He knew that an eagle is king of the sky. He was surprised to see the eagle strutting around the chicken coop, pecking at the ground, and acting very much like a chicken. The farmer explained to the naturalist that this bird was no longer an eagle. He was now a chicken because he had been trained to be a chicken and he believed that he was a chicken.

The naturalist knew there was more to this great bird than his actions showed as he "pretended" to be a chicken. He was born an eagle and had the heart of an eagle, and nothing could change that. The man lifted the eagle onto the fence surrounding the chicken coop and said, "Eagle, thou art an eagle. Stretch forth thy wings and fly." The eagle moved slightly, only to look at the man; then he glanced down at his home among the chickens in the chicken coop where he was comfortable. He jumped off the fence and continued doing what chickens do. The farmer was satisfied. "I told you it was a chicken," he said.

The naturalist returned the next day and tried again to convince the farmer and the eagle that the eagle was born for something greater. He took the eagle to the top of the farmhouse and spoke to him: "Eagle, thou art an eagle. Thou dost belong to the sky and not to the earth. Stretch forth thy wings and fly." The large bird looked at the man, then again down into the chicken coop. He jumped from the man's arm onto the roof of the farmhouse.

Knowing what eagles are really about, the naturalist asked the farmer to let him try one more time. He would return the next day and prove that this bird was an eagle. The farmer, convinced otherwise, said, "It is a chicken."

The naturalist returned the next morning to the chicken farm and took the eagle and the farmer some distance away to the foot of a high mountain. They could not see the farm nor the chicken coop from this new setting. The man held the eagle on his arm and pointed high into the sky where the bright sun was beckoning above. He spoke: "Eagle, thou art an eagle! Thou dost belong to the sky and not to the earth. Stretch forth thy wings and fly." This time the eagle stared skyward into the bright sun, straightened his large body, and stretched his massive wings. His wings moved, slowly at first, then surely and powerfully. With the mighty screech of an eagle, he flew.

(from *Walk Tall, You're A Daughter Of God,* by Jamie Glenn)

If you're surrounded by chickens, that's what you'll become. A lot of chickens are okay being chickens; they will live their entire life sick and tired and flat out miserable and then die one day. Maybe it's because they're too weak or tired or that they don't even know it's possible to change, but for whatever reason, they never do.

Some of us are born into very strong families with Christian bloodlines that go back five or six generations who have been working hard and fighting for the Kingdom, focused on the things that truly matter. Growing up in that dynamic would make it a lot easier to follow Jesus and know your calling because you've seen it modeled out before you.

Of course, nobody's family is perfect and nobody is perfect individually. You can be raised in that environment and still be pulled away by the enemy's schemes and still struggle terribly. But that's his entire plan. Adam and Eve were raised in the breath-takingly beautiful Garden of Eden and had the perfect Father who was perfect in every way. They still fell into the devil's trap of sin and deception, and we're no different today. The devil is constantly trying to attack each and every generation because he knows the stats above I just shared with you.

Maybe you feel "lucky" or "unlucky" as you think about your family tree. After all, you didn't have any say in the family you would be born into. But, remember everyone does the best they can with what they have. Maybe your family members haven't been able to break out of the mess or they have never known how. But here's the thing to focus on—you need to look at the big picture.

God doesn't just care about you and your family. He cares about saving as many people as He can before He sends His Son back here. So instead of thinking, "Why me? Why did I end up in this messed up family?"

Just think, maybe God sent you into your family to break the generational curses that have been on them for generations upon generations. Maybe, perhaps, you're the one who was sent to change the entire trajectory of your family tree. Just as God spoke to me in my bathroom in August of 2020 and told me that I'm stronger than I think I am, I bet He's telling you the exact same thing.

The most common things I see in my clients and followers that have been passed down to them at conception are: abuse, addiction, mental illness, low self-esteem, anger, infidelity, poor financial habits and tons of limiting beliefs. So, if this is you, here's how you begin to rewire and retrain your brain: you must get into a new circle of influence immediately. This doesn't mean you totally desert your family, but you start spending time in better circles of influence. Pray that God brings you a new circle to join and then believe He will do it.

Just as negative things get passed down, so do positive ones. If you were raised by a gentle, calm parent, you probably have taken some of those traits into your own parenting.

If your parents were entrepreneurs and showed you how to take risks and chase after your dreams boldly, then it's probably easier for you to do that as an adult.

If your parents didn't smoke or drink, chances are you probably don't indulge as much as others.

If your parents are happily married and modeled a healthy relationship to you growing up, statistics show that you are likely to model the same to your children.

If you were told from a young age how special and important you are, how uniquely you were created, and that you're the Daughter of the Highest King, you won't settle down with someone who tells you (and treats you) the opposite. You know your worth. You know your value and you are confident in who you are and your abilities.

Higher the Calling, Higher the Attack

If Satan wasn't threatened by you, he would leave you alone. The very fact that he has been after you and your family shows how important you must be to the Kingdom. He knows your identity. He knows you've been called and created on purpose to do damage; that's why he doesn't want you to find that out.

I'm telling you this next part because I don't want his plans to scare you or stall you on your journey out of the valley. The more he sees you connect with God and Godly people, he will begin throwing anything your way, just like a jealous boyfriend who's about to be out of the picture. Your life may start to seem a bit more chaotic and things won't go your way or the way you imagined them going, but just remember: God is in control.

1 Peter 5:8-9 says, "Be sober-minded; be watchful. Your adversary the devil prowls around like a roaring lion, seeking someone to devour. Resist him, firm in your faith, knowing that the same kinds of suffering are being experienced by your brotherhood throughout the world."

Part of staying out of the valley is to learn how to be sober-minded and watchful for the devil's tricks and schemes. He's not as scary as he appears and has no real authority over you. His trick is smoke and mirrors, intimidation, masks, and illusions, so don't let him scare you. Once we learn how to get out of the valley in Part One, I will address how to stay out of The Valley in Part Two.

CHAMELEON

When I was a teenager, my younger sister Hailley got a pet chameleon for her birthday. This may sound kind of strange for your family but for mine, it was just another pet. We always had animals growing up on a farm. Hailley was always attracting every hurt, scared, or injured animal and would rehabilitate them then send them on their way or have a proper burial and funeral for the ones who didn't make it.

We raised a baby skunk, a whole litter of baby opossums, dozens of litters of kittens, puppies, foals, pigs, rabbits, and tons of baby birds. She loved animals—all things soft, furry, creepy, and even crawly. But nothing was like this chameleon who we called Delilah. We had the time of our lives placing Delilah on different pieces of fruit, toys, and surfaces watching her color transform from the red apple to the yellow banana and then blue as she slowly walked onto a pair of thick-framed dollar store sunglasses we picked up that summer for the boat. It was like her entire identity could change in just a few seconds as she turned from bright blue to black and then red all depending on her surroundings and the environment she was in.

Delilah reminds me a lot of myself up until my 30s. In fact, I would say that just in the last couple of years, I stopped molding and transforming into the people around me. If I'm being completely honest, I would say still to this day that I step into a room or into a circle of influence and feel the pull to transform.

This transformation that takes place in humans isn't as beautiful as when it does in a chameleon—it can be messy and devastating. I've seen people lose everything they have based on a bad decision they made by changing colors for the night. I have also almost lost everything myself by a bad circle of influence and I'm sure you probably have to. It's something most of us struggle with from time to time.

Fitting In

When I was a child, I remember wanting to fit in so desperately that I pretended that I needed glasses. My mom made an appointment for me and took me to the town's ophthalmologist. After a brief eye exam, the doctor asked to speak with my mom privately. She knew I was pretending like I couldn't read the letters. So, when glasses didn't work in my favor, I started pretending like I wore contacts to my fellow bus mates turning towards the window and gently pinching my eye and quickly placing my "contact" into the front zipper compartment of my back pack. Some people thought I was lying because I didn't use a mirror to do it, but most of the kids thought I was so cool and that felt amazing.

When I was a about 13 years old, I faked a hickey on my shoulder by giving it to myself and then bragging to all of my friends in the 7th grade that my "boyfriend up north" gave it to me. Why did I think that having a hickey on my shoulder in the 7th grade by a boy would make more people like me even though I was absolutely terrified of boys? I don't know, but it worked. Boys thought I was cool because I was spontaneous, mischievous, and willing—all things I wasn't actually, by the way. The girls thought I was cool because the boys thought so. I later lied about losing my virginity in the 10th grade to—you guessed it—a boy from "up north" just to fit in. Most of my friends had already lost it, or so they said, and I was scared to be labeled weird and a prude for not hooking up with someone, so I lied to fit in.

The thing with being a human chameleon is that the outside doesn't change much (right away) so the change is even harder to spot at first because it happens on the inside.

As a young adult, I would make up entire fake lives about myself as I met different people in bars, clubs, and concerts, all just to fit in and seem exciting. I slowly taught myself over time that nobody liked the real me. Now I can see that it wasn't that they didn't like the real me, it was that they didn't even know the real me. I hid her—well, Satan did, keeping me locked away, having me all to himself and whispering lies in my ear. I saw that I had the ability to make people like me as much as I wanted them to by people-pleasing and blending into my surroundings.

I didn't know my identity back then. I didn't think I was special, set apart, and fearfully and wonderfully made like my Creator had spoken over me. Instead, I listened to the world.

The world says, "Sleep around and get experience. After all, you wouldn't want to end up with someone you didn't have chemistry with." They say, "Have a shot and a few drinks, blow off some steam, you earned it, you had a really hard week." They also are telling us to cheat, to steal, to lie, to do what feels good, to do what feels natural, to do what makes you happy, and to cope with anything that helps us achieve the above goal. It's way easier to do the things you would never do if you're intoxicated or using drugs.

Standing Out

I'm sure you've heard the saying that you become the average of the five people you spend the most time with, so I want you to take a moment and think of who those people are. They don't have to be people you physically are in the same room with. These can be people you are listening to, studying, and watching. If you hang out with a group of negative, overly-critical people, you will find yourself becoming more like them. If you binge watch the Kardashians all day, I'd bet by the end of the day you begin talking and acting like them. But the same goes with good influences too, like good friends who love Jesus and know and love the real you. You might not know the real you right now, but the more you learn your identity in Christ and study what He says about you, the more you will begin to believe it, let down your guard and invite true, genuine relationships into your life.

You need some sisters in Christ. Someone to encourage, relate, and cheer for you. Anyone "of the world" and not of Christ won't understand why you're trying to live set apart from this world and will try to pull you back in unintentionally. They will also try to help you by giving you advice, but unfortunately, it's not the advice you need, like, "Go get laid" or "Drink a bottle of wine" or "Relax and go smoke a joint."

We're not just looking for any person of the same sex who believes in God to befriend. Most people, even Christians, are naturally nay-sayers, looking at the glass as half empty and believing in going with the flow of the majority. But not you. You are made for more and in order to start believing that, you're going to need to hang out with people who also believe the same thing.

I know most of you are first generation followers, meaning no-body else in your family is following Christ like you, which makes it incredibly difficult to live holy and set apart with the constant temp-tation of sin around. Whether you have a person or not, I'm going to be here for you when you're feeling overwhelmed, frustrated, or the day isn't going your way... I want you to pick up this book, turn your own brain off, and listen to these words. You can't listen and talk at the same time, so one of my favorite ways to mute out the devil and step out of the valley is to simply turn his voice off by turning something wholesome and pure on.

Do you have someone that you can call when you're having a hard day and they can lift you up with scripture and encouragement? If not, add to your prayer list for God to connect you to like-minded people and pray this daily. I was so alone and desperate to find my tribe and after praying this prayer over and over again, God started connect-ing me to my soul sisters.

These types of friends can calm you down, talk some sense into you, give you good advice, and pray with you. You'll notice your blood pressure coming down with your rage, your breathing getting a little slower and you begin feeling much better after talking with them. But imagine how much more God could help you.

Trust

God created you and knit you together in your mother's womb. God is the only one who can get you out of the valley. He is the strongest one with the most authority who knows you better than you know yourself, loves you more than anyone else does, and knows the exact steps to take for a direct path out of the valley, the quickest way possible.

God can be trusted and relied on. I know that's hard for so many of us to wrap our heads around, especially since we've never found anyone we can fully rely on and trust in this world. Nobody is perfect and everyone will let you down, it's just a matter of time. But you can trust in Jesus to carry you through the storm.

By the time you're done reading this book, you will be well on your way to living a life of complete fulfillment, joy, and freedom by trusting and depending on Christ fully to carry you out of the valley and into your calling. This book isn't just about being well and escaping the grip of the devil by his fingertips, but instead to equip you to rise to the top of the highest peak and live your life that you have been called to live by Christ to the fullest. You were created on purpose for a purpose. He has a plan for your life, to prosper, not just "get by" or survive.

Fruits of the Spirit

Just as good friends can rub off on you, so can Jesus. When you hang out with Jesus regularly; studying the Word, praying, and listening, you actually start to become more like Him. This is called the fruit of the spirit and it's talked about in *Galatians 5:22 (ESV)*: *"But the fruit of the Spirit is love, joy, peace, patience, kindness, goodness, faithfulness, gentleness, and self-control."*

If you're spending time intimately with Him, this is the fruit people will see in your life that shows you are different because Christ dwells within you.

Transformation

I used to refer to myself as "the Hulk Mom" because of the way I would lose it on my kids. I had ZERO patience. I was not gentle in the way I spoke, I did not have joy or peace in any way, I wasn't very kind, had little to no self-control, and I was not spending time with the Lord. After hitting rock bottom and hearing God tell me to draw closer to Him, that's when everything changed. I went from the green nine-foot-tall angry mom with veins shooting down my arms and neck to a mother who resembled Jesus' mother, Mary—a soft-spoken, gentle, calm, forgiving, patient, and peaceful Mom. The most important thing for me to tell you is that this wasn't my doing. The Holy Spirit changed me because God was one of the five "people" I was spending the most time with.

If you can describe yourself as a Hulk Mom or another villain towards your children, family, or co-workers... Then maybe it's time you kick it up a notch with your time spent with Jesus and watch Him transform your life.

Another thing that really changed in me by spending time with The Lord was the joy I began to feel. Joy is different from happiness. I spent years crying to my husband John, telling him how all I wanted was to be happy. I didn't know that it was joy I actually craved. The main difference between the two is that happiness is triggered by something external while joy happens internally. For example, we can feel happy when we receive something like a gift or achieve something like awards or honors. These things are external or belong to the surface of our lives. It is not something deeper, but rather, superficial. Joy, on the other hand, is something deeper. It is something we feel internally in our lives as human beings. For example, when we feel great joy when we worship God the Father and when we feel great joy when we remember our Lord Jesus Christ dying on the cross to save us from sins.

We naturally have this longing to fit in, to be accepted, to feel needed and wanted. This deep-down yearning to belong was designed in us to turn us to Jesus. That is why nothing can satisfy us here on this earth because we weren't made to be satisfied by earthly things, but eternal things only.

Connection

What God gave us was a desire for community and connection. We're living in a world where we're supposed to be more connected to others by all of these social media outlets but actually studies have found people feeling lonelier now than they ever have before.

Growing up, we didn't have cell phones that could access Facebook, Instagram, and Tik Tok. Heck, we didn't even have those platforms at all. I cannot imagine growing up with the constant comparison, the constant pull to be someone else, the constant desire to achieve and have something else because of what you see others doing and having. I know how it makes me feel as a 33-year-old adult, and let me tell you, it is not good. I am way more mature and established in my identity and calling than a 13-year-old girl.

The devil for sure has a plan with all of this social media and "connection," but rest assured, God also has a plan! Don't let social media become one of your "five" that you hang out with the most.

If you have children, I want to say this to you: The deeper you get in connection with your Creator, the more you learn, the more time you spend with Him, the more you talk to Him and follow His instructions for your life, the better mom you will be. The more equipped you will be to raise your kids in this crazy world. So don't get overwhelmed by all that you have to do and teach your children, but instead, focus on growing God in you and everything else will naturally fall into place, I promise. If you spend time with Jesus, you will begin to act more and more like Him every single day.

That is the goal.

Influencer vs. Influenced

God wants you confident in your identity so that when you're with others out in the world, your chameleon colors influence others to become more like you are instead of the other way around. You are meant to be an influencer, a light, an encourager, pointing people towards the source of life.

I don't want you to think that you need to end every worldly relationship that you're in and only spend time with God and His people. Jesus wants us to model how He lived when He was alive on the earth, and yes, He spent a lot of time praying and talking with God, but He spent even more time with people. He knew how broken the world was and how they needed to learn about His Father through Him.

"You must influence them; do not let them influence you!" Jeremiah 15:19 instructs us.

Hebrews 10:24 says: *"And let us consider how to stir up one another to love and good works, not neglecting to meet together, as is the habit of some, but encouraging one another, and all the more as you see the Day drawing near."*

He knew that the darkness would begin to grow and spread in this world and that the devil would be working hard day and night to divide, steal, and destroy. That is why He instructs us to meet together often, build one another up and pray for each other. He instructs us to get into good circles of influence for protection and safety against the enemy. Just as a sheep wanders away and then is left defenseless to predators, the same goes for you. That is why we have a Shepard and are told to belong to a church. Church is not a building but a group of Christians coming together to do life. Remember though, no church is perfect because it is filled with broken people. Just because someone goes to church does not mean they're a good influence. We're looking for mature Christians to circle up with. You will not move closer to Christ or become more like Christ by circling up with carnal, worldly, poorly influential Christians.

"Walk with the wise and become wise; associate with fools and get in trouble" (Proverbs 13:20 [ESV]).

Application

Before I move onto the next chapter, I want to give you some helpful information and tools to help you grow in this area of your life. If you don't belong to a church and attend Sunday service regularly, you need to start with that. You do not need to go to church in order to get into Heaven, just like you don't need to spend time at home to be married, however, both relationships will suffer if you don't. If the Holy Spirit has already laid a church on your heart to visit or attend, then start there. If you don't have a clue where to start, search for churches in your area and go church hopping! Make sure to pray that the Spirit guides you to wherever you are called to be and then make it a non-negotiable for your *entire family* on Sundays. Our rule is that if we are in town, we go to church, no ifs ands or buts about it.

At first, your kids (and maybe even husband) will give you grief about it, but I promise, after they see your commitment and unwavering expectation, they will eventually stop complaining and begging to skip.

On the subject of husbands, my husband would not under any circumstance come to church with me and the kids at first. He always had "something to do" and when there were no chores or jobs left to be done, he would need to sleep in because he had worked so hard that week and just needed to rest. Continue to ask him every single Sunday and when he says, "no." Do not give him an attitude, eye roll, snarky comment, or sign of disgust. Ask the Spirit to help you do this, to control your mouth, your eyes, and body language. Ask the Spirit to help you act the way Jesus would act towards your husband.

The second thing you need to do is pray every single day for God to speak to him, soften his heart, call to him, and work on changing him AND make sure you ask for Him to change you as well. Pray that any resentment goes away and you're able to respect him and love him while he sorts out his relationship with God. Remember, the issue here is a heart issue, and you're not going to get him to attend church with you by being rude, short, disrespectful, and unloving. That is not showing the love of Jesus. You want to pray for him and then show him how Jesus is changing you. That is what will make him also begin to change. This worked with my husband, and I've seen it work with tons of others.

Get Plugged In

After you find a church, you need to plug into it. There's a difference between being a consumer of church and being plugged in. I spent all of my life as a consumer at my church and it wasn't until a few years ago where I realized I needed to get plugged in and begin to serve. Since then, I have gained so many soul sisters and brothers, good influential mature Christians who are real, honest, open, and love the Lord and model their life after His as much as they can. This shows how when you surround yourself with positive people who are good influences on you, you become that. Your chameleon colors morph into those around you.

Those people I've connected deeply with at my church over the last few years have been a major influence on my life, relationships, mental health, marriage, dreams, goals, parenting, and more. Check with the church and see what they have for new people trying to connect. Depending on the church you're in, they could have tons of different classes, events, and groups. Join one of these and get to know some people and get your kids plugged in the same way now. The devil is already after your kids, and you need them surrounded by as many mature and healthy Christians—AKA good chameleons—as possible to rub off on them.

"Two are better than one, because they have a good reward for their toil. For if they fall, one will lift up his fellow. But woe to him who is alone when he falls and has not another to lift him up! Again, if two lie together, they keep warm, but how can one keep warm alone? And though a man might prevail against one who is alone, two will withstand him—a threefold cord is not quickly broken" (Ecclesiastes 4:9-12 [ESV]).

SELF-WORTH

This could very well be the most impactful chapter you read in this book if you struggle with self-worth, so let's start by defining what self-worth is and what it's not. Self-worth is the internal sense of being good enough, worthy of love, and belonging from others. Self-worth is often confused with self-esteem, which relies on external factors such as successes and achievements to define worth and can often be inconsistent leading to someone struggling with feeling worthy.

Let's dive a little deeper into that word "worthy." Worthy by definition tends to fall under the premise of being good, moral, upright, holding to honesty and respectable living. If we're being honest, none of us are worthy. Not one single person is free from sin. Not one single person is honest all of the time. Not one single person can be "good enough" for God's standards. He says in Romans 3:23, *"For all have sinned and fall short of the glory of God"* and in Romans 3:10, He says, *"As it is written: "None is righteous, no, not one."* So, although you can try your hardest to live a life that is moral, honest, and upright, you're never going to be good enough on your own, that is why we need Jesus.

When we accept Jesus into our hearts and surrender our fleshly desires, and admit we are sinners and cannot change on our own, the Holy Spirit comes to dwell within us. Instead of God turning away from us because He is so holy that He can't even look at sin, He turns towards us and welcomes us into His kingdom for eternity. He doesn't even see a blemish of sin because it has all been washed by the blood of Jesus Christ dying on the cross for us as sinners as a living sacrifice. *Romans 6:23 says, "For the wages of sin is death, but the free gift of God is eternal life in Christ Jesus our Lord."* Praise God!

He knew we would never be good enough for Him, and because of the love in which He loved us, He sent his Son here to die in our place. Let that sink in for a moment. If you're a mom, imagine sending your child to a foreign country that is filled with evil and sin and then allowing your child to be sacrificed for those evil and sinful people so that they would be allowed to spend eternity in your own amazing and perfect country, a place they don't deserve to be.

But we are no different than those people in that foreign country. We are prideful, we are revengeful, we judge and criticize others, we refuse to forgive, we are selfish, we sin all the time doing things we know we shouldn't be doing but we do anyway. We do things like watching porn, cheating on our spouses, getting drunk, and smoking weed. We abuse our prescriptions, tell white lies, and manipulate people to get our own way. We watch shows we shouldn't watch, listen to music we shouldn't be listening to, worship false Gods and idols like money, success, designer purses (fake or real), big checks, promotions, and the list goes on and on and on. Maybe you haven't killed or cheated on anybody, but to God, a sin is a sin. In *1 John 3:15, He says if you hate your brother, you're a murderer. Matthew 5:28 says that if you even look at someone in lust, you have committed adultery.*

So, if you don't feel like you're good enough for God, good. You aren't good enough for God and you never will be. That is why you need His Son, Jesus Christ.

If you've asked the Holy Spirit to dwell within you and you've admitted you're a sinner and can't get into heaven by being good enough, then you're on the perfect track. The devil, however, is going to constantly try to get you to think you're not good enough and get you to focus on yourself, your short-comings and your sins, therefore hiding from God just like Adam and Eve did in the garden. We also saw this happen with Jonah when God told him to go to Nineveh. We should never be hiding from God.

Maybe you grew up with people telling you that you weren't good enough, you didn't have good enough grades, you weren't pretty enough, you weren't skinny enough, you weren't funny enough, and you weren't smart enough. You were too loud, too quiet, too shy, too outgoing, too annoying, too weird, or too boring. Wherever you heard this, whether from family members, classmates, coworkers, boyfriends, or the devil, it wasn't the truth about you. But what happened is that over time you started believing it, and it actually kept you from the close intimate relationship with Jesus that He's been desperate to have with you.

Self-Talk

Valuing my self-worth came after I truly started believing in who He said I was. Before that, I believed the lies and honestly didn't like myself at all. I started speaking the lies to myself, repeating negative self-talk over and over on repeat in my mind like a broken record. "I'm so fat, I'm so annoying, I'm so dumb, I'm always changing my mind, I'm so indecisive, I'm flaky, I'm inconsistent, nobody likes me, I'm ugly, nobody will ever love me, nobody understands me, I'm crazy, I'm weird." This caused me to isolate myself from others, which is exactly the position the devil wanted me in.

If the negative self-talk in my head wasn't bad enough, I started complaining out loud about these things to my friends and family members. What happens when you go from thinking to speaking is actually a huge step in the wrong direction for several reasons.

The first reason is that instead of just thinking it in your brain, you're now speaking it out loud, hearing it, and then thinking about it. It is now affecting you three times more than it was. Every single time you say something negative about yourself, you believe it more and more. I don't know if people are still spewing negativity about you and telling you who you are or if that was something you only dealt with as a child, but here's my advice: Promise yourself that you will begin to love yourself and see yourself the way that God sees you by not letting a single negative word about yourself cross your lips. Now your thoughts are a little harder to control but what you're going to do is write down another prayer.

It should sound something like this:

"Lord, help me to start seeing myself through your eyes and hearing myself through your ears. Help me to look in the mirror and begin seeing the woman you say that I am—chosen, anointed, set apart, beautiful, special, unique, called, righteous, forgiven, and holy. Bury this deep down in my soul so that I never forget it and I am able to love myself the way that you love me."

Another reason that you shouldn't be spewing hate out loud towards yourself is because the devil can now hear you and knows your weaknesses. He can't read your mind, so when you're thinking these things, he doesn't know it and cannot use it against you to attack you and bring you down. Once he knows what you think because you keep telling people and talking about it, then it's game on. Remember his plan is to steal, kill, and destroy everything in your life by getting you to think you don't need God, you don't need His people, and you can do it alone. When you get into this mindset, he has you right where he wants you—all to himself.

Toxic Relationships

If you are currently in a situation where you are surrounded by people talking down to you or about you, you need to set a healthy boundary and let them know you will no longer allow them to speak like that to you. Quick side note: If this is your husband, it's a little different of a situation since you can't just leave, but I would definitely seek further help and assistance from your local church, Christian counselor or abuse counselor immediately—today. Physical and verbal abuse is never okay, and although God says He hates divorce, He hates abuse just as much. You do not need to stay in any abusive relationship just because you're married, especially with children involved, because all it's doing is creating more generational sin, curses, and brokenness to pass down. If you can't do it for yourself, do it for them. Now, divorce isn't something I recommend because that has its own issues and brokenness that follow, however, abuse is one of the two reasons God says is valid for divorce or separation.

If the person spewing hate and negativity to you is a family member, it's perfectly understandable to separate them from your life, even if they're your mother, your father, your sibling or your best friend since childhood. When we're kids, we don't have a choice of who we're around and what happens, but as an adult you definitely do. You don't have to be hateful back, and most of the time you don't even have to have the conversation with them, just simply start distancing yourself from them. Most of the time, they get the picture.

If it is a close family member that you're trying to distance from, then I would recommend in most cases having a conversation to let them know you will no longer allow negativity into your life or your family's life from them, and if it doesn't stop you, will be ending the relationship. If you live with this person, you need to start praying that God opens a door to help you escape the abuse. Toxic relationships are never okay and sometimes are hard to identify, especially if that's all you've ever known. To identify if a relationship is toxic or not, ask yourself how you feel after leaving their presence. If you don't leave feeling good and refreshed, then it could be a sign the relationship is toxic. Pray that God separates them from your life and then when He starts to, just let it go and focus on Jesus instead of the negativity that comes from the imploding friendship/relationship. Usually if someone is toxic, verbally abusive, mentally abusive, or physically abusive, when you try to create that boundary, they will bust right through it. There have been a ton of relationships I have had to end because of this. Not all of them were extreme, but I decided I was no longer going to let people around me create any kind of negativity. I once had a best friend who I constantly found myself walking on eggshells around, over-thinking everything I did or said, and I felt manipulated. It took some time, but eventually we went our separate ways, and the only way I could do it was to quit my job since that is something we shared. I had other co-workers and bosses that were extremely negative, manipulative, and even narcissistic that I had to walk away from also.

You must protect yourself and ask God to protect you and separate you from these people because it will make it ten times harder to grow and become who God wants you to be with them around. Eventually, you will find yourself living a life that fills you up and lifts you up by the people you've allowed into it. I can honestly say that today I have nobody in my friendship circle, my family, my household, or my work that spews hate towards me, make me feel less than, manipulated, triggered, or uncomfortable. Today, I would never stand for that, but I once did. The difference now is that I am 100% confident in who I am, who I belong to and what God says about me.

I promise you with everything I have, if you keep looking to Jesus you will get there too.

Journal Prompt

The final thing I want to leave you with in this chapter is a journal prompt that I do with mostly all my clients I've coached. Write down 20 things you don't like about yourself. Yes, I said, "don't like."

These can be physical things or mental things, personality traits, you name it... Whatever you hate, write it down. The reason I have you start with this is for two reasons. One, it's easier for people to list what they hate about themselves rather than what they love about themselves. Two, it's incredible how quickly your thoughts about something can change, so when you write it down and date it, it's proof of how you used to think. I reread back through old journals of mine and cannot believe I thought and acted the way I did. Things I used to absolutely hate about myself I now am so in love with.

After you make your negative list about yourself, I want you to take each thing and turn it into a positive statement. For example, if you wrote down that you hate how fat you are, rewrite the sentence to say, "I am in love with my body and how I treat it." Another example for you is if you wrote down how you hate that you're a pushover you can change it to say "I love how strong of a personality I have, never allowing myself to bend or change in areas that I am certain of."

At first, this will feel silly and you'll probably want to hide your journal somewhere nobody will ever see it because writing nice stuff about ourselves feels conceited or made up, but in order to change the narrative in your head, you need to change the message that's going into your brain. You will repeat these positive statements about yourself so that they influence and impact you three times the amount that they would if you just said them in your head and also, you guessed it, say them out loud to let the devil know you ain't playin' anymore.

ROCK BOTTOM

A few years ago, I traveled to the beautiful island of Oahu, Hawaii with my mom and sister, Hunter, to visit my sister, Hailley, who was in the Coast Guard. It was just us girls, and we went for 10 days. It was paradise. The best part about traveling to this island was that my sister had lived there for a couple years, so she knew the ins and outs of the entire island like places to eat and adventures to take that only the locals knew about.

She took us to this place on the edge of the ocean called Mermaid Caves that looked like a whack-a-mole board with tiny openings at the surface that lead down below. You could peek your head down into one of the holes and see nothing but darkness. She was looking for a specific hole that she found before that had a ladder placed inside of it, and once she found it, she told us we were going down. I was absolutely not going down into this dark hole next to the ocean, but she persisted and promised it would be the most beautiful thing I'd ever seen.

I let my mom and sisters go down first, and then once I saw their reactions and that it was safe, I decided I was going to talk myself into it by repeating the mantra, "I can do all things through Christ who gives me strength," which is something I repeat to myself often when trying to do something my brain is fearful of.

I climbed down the shaky ladder as they held it steady for me and carefully stepped off the last step onto the sandy bottom. I followed my sister's light from her phone a couple feet around a corner and then saw the opening. The light was shining in from the ocean and the water was slowly rushing in and out, creating the most beautiful hidden cave I have ever seen. I kept thinking how grateful I was that I walked down into the cave because it was nothing like I thought it would be. I had expected this terrible, scary dark place but it was the furthest place from that.

Sometimes our minds play tricks on us and imagine the worst-case scenario happening, or the other way around where we think things won't be that bad but they turn out way worse than we imagined. The thing about caves is that you never really know where they lead because there's no light shining and showing us the truth about what to believe, leaving everything up to your imagination.

One day while I was journaling a prayer to God, He had me sketch an illustration of The Valley, and this time, He had me include caves below the surface of the Valley floor. They were all different depths and widths, but what they all had in common was that each one held only one person, not because of its lack of size, but because of the way it was strategically designed.

The thing about hitting rock bottom is that every person hits a different "bottom." Some people's rock bottoms are losing their entire family, their job, their house, their dignity, their friends, and everything they've ever loved and cared about. Others feel they've hit rock bottom once they realize the addiction has just started getting out of hand and they decide to seek help.

In my illustration, I drew a picture of the devil at the bottom of the page and a picture of God at the top. In the middle, I drew peaks and valleys of a mountain with the caves below the valley floor and the clouds and sun up above the peaks by God. I am no artist and very rarely draw anything, but this image came so quickly I was sketching as fast as I could. I immediately noticed when I was finished that the caves were insanely close to the devil, and it made me think: When we are at our own rock bottom, it is as if we are "trapped" in this cave. It is dark, we feel all alone, and we are so close to the devil that we can hear his whispers to us the loudest. Because there's nobody else in there with us, it's insanely quiet and we feel we can't escape our own thoughts or the ones being placed inside of our heads by our adversary.

I say we "feel" all alone because we're never actually truly alone. God is always right there with us; He never will desert you or abandon you. That doesn't mean that sometimes you won't feel like He has, especially in the grips of addiction, depression, isolation, or anger.

So why does rock bottom feel so lonely? Because it's all part of the devil's plan to isolate you, pull you down, and make you feel like you are the only person going through what you're going through, suffocating you in shame and guilt. Even though there are people down in caves to your right and to your left, you can't see them or hear them because society has made it a norm to not talk about that kind of stuff.

In recent years, opening up about depression or mental illness has grown to be more acceptable, but just a few decades ago, if you talked about mental illness, you were sure to end up admitted into a psych ward immediately.

Your Environment

So, you're down in the cave and you feel alone, the devil has completely isolated you and is shouting these lies into your head about who you are and whose you are, making you feel very far from being chosen and anointed. Remember that you become the average of the five people you're spending the most time with. I have found this saying to be true time and time again, especially for people "trapped" in the cave. The only thing you're hearing is the devil. I say "trapped" like this because you're not actually really trapped. In Luke 3:10, Jesus is quoted saying, *"Behold, I have given you authority to tread on serpents and scorpions, and over all the power of the enemy, and nothing shall hurt you."* It's like you're in a jail cell that appears to be shut and locked with a shackle attached to your ankle that appears to be locked as well. It also appears that you're all alone in there and there's no hope or no way out. In fact, a lot of people die in there, suffering and waiting for someone to come and rescue them. Although Jesus already came to rescue you, He is not going to force you to leave because He is love, and love doesn't force, but it flows of free will. So, the entire picture is really just smoke and mirrors. The door is not locked, it's not even shut! And the shackle—yep! That too is not locked on your ankle; all you have to do is jiggle it, and it falls right to the ground.

Nobody is waiting outside of the door to restrain you once you start to walk out, either. You can just swing open the door and begin your journey to freedom. That is literally all it takes to get out of the cave, but the devil's greatest scheme is getting you to think you can't. That's it. If he can get you to believe that you're hopeless, he wins. But what does God say about all of this?

Let's take a look.

Psalm 34:17-20 (ESV) says, *"When the righteous cry for help, the Lord hears and delivers them out of all their troubles. The Lord is near to the brokenhearted and saves the crushed in spirit. Many are the afflictions of the righteous, but the Lord delivers him out of them all. He keeps all his bones; not one of them is broken."*

He also says in Jeremiah 29:11 (ESV), *"For I know the plans I have for you, declares the Lord, plans for welfare and not for evil, to give you a future and a hope."* This is why it is crucial you start to memorize scripture and store it up in your heart so that you never forget what has already been spoken over you.

Spiritual Weapons

Memorizing scripture is a spiritual weapon. "The sword of the Spirit" is just one of the weapons we have been given that God describes in the book of Ephesians. Quoting scripture and prayer are the only offensive weapons we have—all the other ones have been given us as defensive weapons.

In Ephesians 6:13-17, He describes all of the weapons you have been given: *"Therefore, put on the full armor of God, so that when the day of evil comes, you may be able to stand your ground, and after you have done everything, to stand. Stand firm then, with the belt of truth buckled around your waist, with the breastplate of righteousness in place, and with your feet fitted with the readiness that comes from the gospel of peace. In addition to all this, take up the shield of faith, with which you can extinguish all the flaming arrows of the evil one. Take the helmet of salvation and the sword of the Spirit, which is the word of God."*

You may have heard this scripture broken down or even completed a study on the *Armor of God*, but if you haven't, I highly recommend Priscilla Shirer's study called *The Armor of God*. I want to quickly break down what each of these weapons are designed for because Ephesians 6:12 says, *"For our struggle is not against flesh and blood, but against the rulers, against the authorities, against the powers of this dark world and against the spiritual forces of evil in the heavenly realms."*

The scripture first describes the Belt of Truth, and since Satan is the father of lies and deception is high on his list, it is crucial that we be truthful in everything we say and do so he doesn't think we follow him. This also goes with what you hear. Satan is always putting lies in my head about my identity, and I bet he's doing that to you too. So, the next time you're feeling worthless, stupid, inconsistent, not good enough, fearful, or fill in the blank, I want you to look online to see what scripture says about being "good enough" or fill in whatever you're struggling with. When I'm looking up scriptures, I like to click on the link for the site called www.openBible.info because there are no ads and all of the scripture is very easy to read one after the other.

Next, we have the Breastplate of Righteousness. A breastplate in an armor suit is used to shield your vital organs. This righteousness is not of our own doing but of God's righteousness to protect your inner most vital part of your body from the enemy, your soul. If you believe God will protect you and hold onto that truth, He will. It doesn't matter what the enemy throws at you, or even if he kills you because he cannot touch your soul. *"Oh death, where is your sting?"* (*1 Corinthians 15:55*).

Next in the scripture, He mentions the Shoes of Peace. As you attempt to follow down the path God has laid out for you, Satan will have set traps for you everywhere. But don't let that discourage you. God has given you the Shoes of Peace to help you walk in peace! If you begin to focus too much on the attacks the devil has planned, it will rob your peace. Our confidence should be in Jesus 100% to get us through the storms and traps.

Next, we have The Shield of Faith. Satan will always sow seeds of doubt about the faithfulness of God and get into your head and make you think that His word is ineffective. *Hebrews 12:2 says Christ is the Author and the perfector.* Just like a shield is solid and substantial, your faith can be the same.

The Helmet of Salvation is one of the most important pieces of Armor and here's why. The helmet offers protection for the head, an extremely critical part of the body. The head is the seat of the mind and when it has laid hold of the gospel truths of hope and eternal life. It will not receive false doctrine or give way to Satan's temptations. The unsaved person has no hope of warding off the blows of false doctrine because she is without the helmet of salvation and her mind is incapable of discerning between spiritual truth and spiritual deception. If you've said the sinner's prayer and you truly believe, then you have the helmet of salvation. If you're wondering whether or not you have your helmet on, it's best to be safe than sorry and say the prayer again.

Here, I'll even lead us:

"Lord, we want your helmet of salvation and every piece of armor you have that is available to us to fight off the devil. We know you sent your Son down to earth as a human man to die on the cross for our sins as a living sacrifice so that we would never be separated from you and our souls would spend eternity with you. I believe this, Lord, and I know I can't do this without you. Holy Spirit; come into my soul and walk with me day by day. Teach me how to change my ways, renew me and transform me to become more like your Son, Jesus. I want all you have to offer and I love you. Thank you for loving me unconditionally and never giving up on me, Amen."

Next, we have The Sword of the Spirit. As we read previously it is the word of God. His words speak of the Holiness and power of God.

It's important to know that Satan *will* attack you. Not maybe—he will.

In the book of Matthew, it says that after Jesus was baptized by his cousin, John the Baptist: *"... He went up out of the water. At that moment heaven was opened, and he saw the Spirit of God descending like a dove and coming to rest on Him. Then a voice from heaven boomed from the clouds, saying, 'This is my beloved Son, with whom I am well pleased.'"* But immediately after the Bible says that Jesus was led into the wilderness by the spirit to be tempted by the devil. Even Jesus was tempted and lured, so you definitely will not be left alone unless you're not a threat to the devil, but I'm guessing because you're this far into this book that you probably are at this point.

We can learn from Jesus by studying how He dealt with the attack, and He did this by quoting scripture to the devil. He didn't make up his own words—He recited scripture word for word. But it's important to know how the devil responded back because he also responded back in scriptures. That's right! Even the devil knows scripture so don't let him deceive you and trick you.

Last but certainly not least, we have prayer as one of the offensive weapons against the enemy. We cannot neglect prayer; it's where we draw spiritual strength from God. Without prayer, without reliance upon God, our efforts at spiritual warfare are none. So, if you struggle with what to pray, you can print out my prayer list as well by going to www.tarrynsarcone.com/TheValley

Valley or Peak?

Now that you know the weapons that are in your arsenal, it's time you recognize that the devil has held you captive long enough and it's time you break out of the cell and leave the valley. After all, you've already read the end of the story. You know that "the good guys," AKA Team God, wins in the end.

If you're not sure if you're currently at rock bottom in the valley, then take a few minutes and think about the following questions.

- Do you often feel worthless, hopeless, or numb?
- Is your life lacking joy?
- Do you struggle believing in who God says you are?
- Do you think awful things about yourself?
- Do you hate yourself?
- Are you coping or self-medicating in an attempt to feel better?
- Do you regularly punish yourself for the sins you've committed?
- Is your environment surrounded with toxic people?
- Have you felt isolated from the world?
- Do you often feel you're not enough?
- Do you wonder if the world would be better off without you?
- Have you felt you're physically in a room but mentally far away?
- Are your emotions unbalanced where you feel irritated, depressed, overwhelmed, or anxious for no reason at all?
- Is your self-care poor?
- Do you often feel sick and tired?
- Have you been neglecting important relationships?
- Have you been neglecting time with God?
- Do you have trauma you haven't healed from?
- Do you struggle with anger/rage?
- Does your mind race with worry and fear?

If you answered yes to most of these, you're in the valley, but don't let this get you down. Admitting you're in the valley/prison cell and have been captured mentally will be your first step to freedom.

Imagine your life filled with hope for the future, joy so deep you cry and feel as if you could burst. You know exactly who you were created to be and from which bloodline you come. You truly believe you're the Daughter of the Highest King and that you are chosen, set apart and anointed to do big things. You know your purpose and your life is immersed in it. You love who you are and you love lifting others up when you're around them. You can remain still and trust in God, letting all worry and fear leave your body. You aren't triggered or lash out because you're healed from your past. You feel present and focused in each area of your life. You would describe yourself as abundant, free, and fulfilled. You're at the Peak.

Now, that may seem so far off from the truth, but it only took six months for God to completely turn my life around once I started obeying Him. That list I just gave above was my list—exactly how I used to feel in the Valley. I got it straight out of my journal. I'm sharing because I want you to have hope that you're not too far gone and abundance, joy and fulfillment aren't that far away.

As I'm in the final edits of this book, I'm adding in that "today" I'm on the peak. I think it was just two days ago that I felt I was headed back into a Valley. I'm telling you this because I want you to know what to expect so you don't feel crazy and alone when you get there. I want you prepared for what's ahead: to keep you in the light and to help guide you down the path God has for your life. Just because you start walking out of the valley does not mean it's smooth sailing from here. The second part of this book has a specific purpose: to climb out of the valley. Part Two will identify the red flags in life that tell us "we're headed into the valley again." The sooner we know, the better.

PART 2

ASCENDING

Before I dive deep into Part 2, I want to congratulate you for getting this far in the book. Most people never finish a book, so the fact that you're more than half way through is admirable. The first half of this book was teaching you who you are and empowering you to get up and get moving. The second half of the book helps you climb out. With each chapter you're going to get higher and higher on the mountain, further out of the valley and feel better and better, so keep reading.

You're also going to need constant reminders on how to handle a specific problem; mindset, self-worth, self-sabotage, identity, proactive living, etc., so please go back to each chapter and re-read as needed. This book is not designed to just read through once and be done, but instead it's a guide or a map, if you will, to pull back out and remember the way. Even I, the writer of this book and Valley expert, need reassurance of these things because occasionally I fall into the valley for a day or two but because I know the way out, I bounce back pretty quickly, which is exactly what I want for you.

REWIRING YOUR BRAIN

When I was in the fifth grade, we had a program called D.A.R.E at our elementary school that stood for Drug Abuse Resistance Education that helped educate children about alcohol and drugs and how it affects your brain, body, and life. To prove their point on alcohol consumption and how it greatly affects your judgment, vision, focus and balance, they called us down to an assembly in the gym and asked for volunteers to try on the "drunk goggles." Almost everyone's hand shot up, including mine, for a chance to experience what adults got to experience. I say it like that because when you're a kid and you've never experienced alcohol like you've seen your parents, grandparents, uncles or other family members experience it, it seems like you're missing out. But if like me, you grew up and indulged in a few too many alcoholic beverages and experienced the loss of balance, spinning room, nausea, and vomiting that comes with being intoxicated, then you know that nobody is "missing out" on this feeling.

One by one, we were called up, the goggles strapped to our faces, and we had to walk through an obstacle course of small orange cones to a table, pick something up, and walk back. No child did this successfully, even though they promised they could. Whoever completed the obstacle course without knocking over any cones received a stuffed animal lion wearing a small black D.A.R.E T-shirt, so there was a lot riding on this to a fifth grader.

What's interesting about this exercise is that everyone thought they could complete the task with no problem at all, but what they didn't realize is that once those goggles were on, your entire world changed. The way you viewed it, the way your brain worked and felt, the way you balanced, your focus—everything.

I often think of these goggles when I am experiencing different emotions in my life of motherhood and just being a woman who sometimes feels like she's strapped to the hormone rollercoaster at a theme park. Have you ever been so angry that you actually saw red? Or maybe you saw black and your vision started to go away. Or maybe you were so angry that you did something out of character—you said something, you hit someone, you threw something—something you did in that moment is something you never would have done in a calmer emotion.

Emotional Lenses

Emotions are extremely important to pay attention to and identify because they are the goggles that you are wearing at any given moment. When you're feeling hopeless and overwhelmed, there's not a whole lot you can do while you're in that emotion, even though you think there is. You won't solve your problems, improve your marriage, be a better parent, overcome challenges at work or take steps closer to achieving your God-given dreams and visions. Actually, the opposite happens, and you end up doing more damage if you don't learn to identify which emotion you're currently in and then take the steps to get out of it.

The following are different emotions people generally find themselves experiencing listed from the lowest possible emotion to the best. This list can be found by going to www.tarrynsarcone.com/TheValley but it is not my own. Dr. Hicks came up with this emotional scale and I have used it faithfully over the years. I highly recommend printing out a copy and taping it somewhere you can easily refer to.

1. Fear/Grief/Depression/Despair/Hopelessness
2. Insecurity/Guilt/Unworthiness
3. Jealousy
4. Hatred/Rage
5. Revenge
6. Anger
7. Discouragement
8. Blame
9. Worry
10. Doubt
11. Disappointment
12. Overwhelm
13. Frustration/Irritation/Impatience
14. Pessimism
15. Boredom
16. Contentment
17. Hopefulness
18. Optimism
19. Positive expectation/Belief

20. Enthusiasm
21. Passion
22. Joy/Empowerment/Freedom/Love/Abundance

Let me explain how this works. For starters, if you don't know what one of these emotions means, it sometimes helps to look up the definition. Begin by deciding where you are currently at. Now, since you're in the middle of reading this book, I can almost guarantee you are at a nine (worry) or higher on the scale of emotions. You may have been below a nine experiencing hatred/rage or depression earlier today or the day before, but usually people who are currently in those low emotions aren't reaching for a book, they're reaching for a bottle of alcohol, a joint, THC gummy, food, their credit card, sex, sleep, or are obsessively scrolling through social media on their phones or some-thing equal in destruction and distraction against the real problem. They're not reading a book that will improve their life. As humans, we want to numb the emotions and pain as quickly as we can so we "feel better." These things will help you to feel better in the moment, but I promise, after the moment passes, the problem is actually magnified now. I'm going to teach you a way to actually feel better and move your emotions up the scale step by step.

So, let's say you're currently feeling a nine emotion of worry, and it really doesn't matter if you know why or you don't know why. All that matters is you are able to identify where you are. Don't overthink this. Next, look at the next emotion you see on the list above this one, which is doubt. Now what I'm going to tell you to do is going to sound silly and you may be thinking, "Tarryn, this is not going to work." But I promise you that it will. Not only have I been doing this for years, but Dr. Hicks has also taught a lot of other people to do the same. I want you to think about, or even write down (if you're a visual person) all of the things you're doubting right now—the more doubts, the better. Go ahead and do this and pick the book back up once you're done.

Did you do it? If not, make sure you do this when you're desperate to change your emotional state and feel better, or re-read this chapter at that time again. But either way make sure you print off or take a screenshot of the Emotional Scale from my website.

After you have written down all of the things you are currently doubting, I want you to look at the next emotion on the scale which is Disappointment. What are you disappointed in right now? What is really letting you down? Make a list of everything you can think about and move on again. The next emotion higher on the scale is overwhelm and you guessed it, we're going to be making a list of everything that is causing us to feel overwhelmed.

This might make you feel more discouraged, disappointed, or overwhelmed once you shed light on where those emotions are coming from, but we're working on shifting your perspective right now in order to rewire your brain. Although feeling worried, doubtful, and overwhelmed are all negative emotions, feeling overwhelmed is better than feeling doubtful, and feeling doubtful is better than feeling worried. It's overwhelming to think, "Okay so I'm depressed, and I need to become joyful. How am I ever going to make such a drastic change in my life?!" This helps you take one step at a time. So, instead of thinking of the emotion all the way at the other end of the scale, we're just trying to go from depressed to insecure. Make sense?

Once you write down all the things overwhelming you, go up the scale again and make a list of the things you're feeling impatient about (one of my favorite lists to make that really improves my emotions). One quick thing about impatience is that you can't trust in God and be impatient at the same time. By being impatient you're basically doubting God's plan and that's a plan you either trust in, or you don't.

If you struggle with patience towards achieving your goals, then write down a prayer in your prayer journal and ask God to help you grow in your patience and to help you to trust in his plan, process, and time.

Remember, you are exactly where you're supposed to be right now. I have this sentence set as the background wallpaper of my laptop as the constant reminder. God's timing is absolutely perfect. In Habbakuk 2:3 it says, *"For still the vision awaits its appointed time; it hastens to the end—it will not lie. If it seems slow, wait for it; it will surely come; it will not delay."*

After you have your complete list of all the things you're sick of waiting for, make a list and shift your focus to pessimism. What are all the things you are feeling negative about? Go ahead, make a full list of every single thing you can think of (the more things you list, the better) and get it all out.

After pessimism, you're going to shift to boredom. Boredom is a neutral emotion and is actually really good to identify. A lot of times when I sit down to do this activity, I find myself in a place of boredom and actually find a lot of comfort in that. I think as humans in this century, it's easy for us to feel bored. In a world where anything is available and possible, every single thing is within your reach if you want it badly enough, it's hard to decide what you even want to begin with. If you can decide what you want, it's hard to stay focused on that one thing because there are so many things competing for our attention and our time. This book is competing for your attention right now. Your chores and to do list, your family, your job, your friends are all competing. Not to mention Facebook, Instagram, Tik Tok, Twitter, LinkedIn, your email, the news, all your apps, and the list goes on and on and on, never ending. So, the minute (or I should probably say second) something loses your interest, you're immediately on to the next thing whether you know what it is or you're still searching to find it.

Our culture has made boredom to be a bad thing, but I once read a book that spoke on this topic and said how the lack of boredom we now experience is ruining our creativity and our passions. So many children learned to play guitar out of boredom at their grandma's house with nothing to do, so they picked it up and began to learn. They also spoke about creating art by doodling out of boredom, drawing, or painting. So many talented people are out there who don't even know it. You may be one of these people who is naturally gifted at musical instruments, art, design, fashion, humor, writing, or one of the other thousands of gifts, but you never know it because you've never allowed yourself to be bored enough for long enough to find out.

Boredom is good. It's neutral. It's relaxing, quiet, and calm. When you look at boredom, it seems a heck of a lot better than depression, revenge, worry, or even doubt. So, soak it up. Boredom is good, but it's not where we will remain forever. Try shifting your perspective from boredom to contentment, and instead of thinking of all the things you're bored with, think of all the things you are content with in your life. What are the things that are going pretty well? Make a complete list in your journal.

So, as you see, shifting your perspective can be very easy if you take it one step at a time. Anytime you find yourself totally freaking out, feeling despair, stress, worry or any other emotion, stop and come back to this chapter, identify which number on the scale you're at, and then work step by step to bring yourself to a new emotional state.

It's extremely important to remember that you have emotions, and they are normal and common to every single human being, but you are not your emotion. Emotions come and go, they never last forever. If you find yourself unable to slide up the scale step by step because your emotions are overcoming you, don't beat yourself up. Remember, we are trying to rewire our brain and this will take time.

So, in this case, my recommendation is to take a nap. Honestly. Cancel your plans for the day and go to sleep. Sleeping will neutralize your emotions and chances are you're probably tired anyway and could use some rest.

Awareness

It's important to identify red flags that we're in the valley because you can't fix the problem if you're not aware of it. You don't want to go days feeling awful, over-thinking, over-analyzing, worrying and stressing, filled with imposter syndrome and doubt allowing fear and worthlessness to take control of you. All of those things do not align with Christ's word. That is why we have to take our thoughts captive like the scripture says in 2 Corinthians 10:5, *"We take captive every thought to make it obedient to Christ."*

Certain days, I wake up with intrusive thoughts depending on my cycle, my hormones, my to-do list, or my health, and the minute I open my eyes to my alarm clock, I'm just grumpy and can tell that today's good day is going to take some work to achieve. But I think that the beautiful part about this is that good days are a choice. I used to think that good days were just completely random and out of my control and if they were good, I'd take them, and if they were bad? Well, I would just drink or cope through them. But actually, there are several things you're going to learn in this book that you can do to change your perspective, your mood, your emotions, and your thoughts. If you wake up not feeling the day, it's okay. You have the power and you'll soon have all of the tools in your tool box to achieve any type of day you want to achieve. You are in control of your emotions, and if you don't feel like you are, you soon will learn to control them.

Stop Listening

One thing I learned early on is that you never want to take advice from someone who is not of sound mind. If your mind isn't sound right now, stop listening to the advice it is giving you; it's as simple as that. And it's not only your voice you're hearing, but also the devil's. He is so good at disguising his voice and sneaking in to whisper lies in your ear. If you can't turn off the negative thoughts and voices, then my advice to you is to drown them out by turning up the volume on the good. You can't listen and talk at the same time, remember? So, when your mind is racing with worry, fear of the unknown, fear of failure, doubt, stress, depression, anxiety, or lack of clarity, the best thing you can do is pick up this book, pick up the Bible, turn on a sermon, or one of my WAKE UP! with Tarryn Sarcone Podcasts and either read out loud or turn up the volume.

But, I want to be realistic because sometimes my depression, my moods, and my emotions are so poor that even the thought of listening to something uplifting annoys me, and in those cases, I cancel my day, turn on Netflix and watch whatever will turn off my mind. I try to nap and give myself grace. Now, if this is happening once a week then you probably are going to want to apply more tools that I give you in this book, especially seeking professional help which we'll discuss later, but it's okay to have a few days like this a month. You definitely will have more of these days in the beginning of your healing journey out of the valley but they will become less and less as your brain reprograms itself.

When I was in the deepest pit of the valley, I would have a few days like this all strung together where I couldn't even leave my bed. I was in deep isolation, and it was not healthy. Maybe this is where you are right now, and if it is, just know you're in good company. I get it. Been there, done that. But this is not where you're going to stay. Taking a mental health day to shut off your brain and rest is completely different than feeling that massive amount of dread, isolation, and avoidance that's keeping you bound in your room, so I want you to understand that there is a difference. Also, something extremely important I need to mention is that when you're feeling this way, you should intentionally isolate yourself from worldly influences around you like social media or people who are non-believers, negative or pessimistic, especially if you consider yourself to be an empath. An empath is someone who has the ability to absorb someone else's energy around them and be hyper aware of how someone else is feeling. This is a blessing and it's also a curse. To have the gifting of walking into a room and connecting with people's energies to know how they're doing, feeling, and what they're experiencing allows you to connect with people on an intimate level, but what happens is that you are trying everything in your own power to keep your energy up and good, and someone comes into your space with a bad energy and immediately it jumps on you.

The best example I can give of this is when you are coming home and you're in a great mood, excited to see your husband and kids, and then you walk through the door and immediately sense the chaos, your husband is yelling at the kids, the kids are in bad moods or crying, and immediately your emotion shifts and you begin yelling. You're over-stimulated and irritated when seconds before you were totally fine.

Blind Spots

This leads me to my next point I want to cover on emotional and perspective lenses. Just like the drunk goggles made me trip and fall over all the cones in the obstacle course, the audience wasn't affected at all.

It is extremely important not only for your emotional health but your spiritual health and even your salvation that you find people in your circle who can see your emotional blind spots. This is when your emotion has completely overtaken you and you're unable to see certain aspects of your life and situations because you're too close to them, therefore it's creating a blind spot. You don't need a friend with some special sort of gifting, all you need is a friend who is a good true friend who loves you for you. Pretty much anyone can spot the blind spots in your life for you if you are honest with them and let them get close enough to you. You may have people like this already in your circle and that is fantastic but if you're reading this thinking, "Yea, Tarryn, that would be great if I had someone like that..."

Then here's my advice to you: Start praying God brings you good, honest, mature people into your circle, your soul sisters who just get you. Write that down on your prayer list if you haven't already so you don't forget to intentionally pray for this daily.

Prayer works best when partnered with action, so you need to go to the places where you'll meet these friends and then put yourself out there. I know. Take a deep breath I promise this gets easier the more you do it and the more you rely on the Holy Spirit to help you achieve this. You can't just lay in bed watching Netflix and hoping a friend knocks on your door and asks you to come outside to play. Although that would be fantastic, it's unrealistic. You have to put yourself out there. Join a church, join a small group, join a team to serve on, and pray that the Spirit leads you to your people. Have you been thinking of joining the hospitality team at your church or serving with the children's ministry? Give it a shot. Maybe it's the Holy Spirit leading you. Maybe you'll meet a friend who's also serving with the children that you end up going to coffee with and getting close and then the two of you join the worship team together or become greeters. Just start praying and get plugged in somewhere so you can find your people sooner than later.

When you meet a sister in Christ who is spiritually mature and healthy, it's amazing how quickly you build trust and connect to them. I think it's because we're deeply connected spiritually, so there's a lot we already know about each other.

Gratitude

The last point I want to make in this chapter is this. Emotions are something to be grateful for, even if they're bad. Bad emotions are telling you how your brain and body are feeling. They're not something to be ignored and brushed under the rug, they're telling you something is wrong. Be grateful for the awareness of the emotion and thank yourself for feeling that way which is protecting you and teaching you something. Anytime you're feeling tension in your life—things aren't going your way, you're in a difficult season, your kids are trying your patience or you're experiencing struggles in your career—remember that you are growing. These are growing pains.

Tension over time equals growth. The only way to learn patience is to be in stressful situations that produce patience. The only way to learn how to be happy is to be unhappy for so long that you reach for books and guidance to learn how to get out like you did with this one.

God is not a genie in a bottle that you can rub and wish for joy and *poof*—joy falls all around you. God will help you and usually when we're in valleys or in dark low emotions, it's an answer to prayer. He is trying to move you further along, teach you life-lessons and grow you into the Daughter He designed you to be.

You are not your emotion, you're just experiencing it and I believe if you apply this chapter to your life, you will be able to rewire your brain and notice a drastic improvement.

PROACTIVE VS. REACTIVE

It was 6:45 in the morning when my alarm clock started going off. I had set it the night before because I wanted to get up an hour earlier than my kids, read my Bible, drink my coffee, and pray. I stayed up until 1:00 am watching a Health Documentary the night before and immediately pressed snooze before the first musical sound came out of my phone. Nine minutes later I pressed snooze again. Nine minutes later, I snoozed again and continued until it was almost 8:00 am. My kids should've been woken up at 7:50 am, so I am now 10 minutes late. I get up and go into my nine-year-old daughter's room and begin the wake up process for her, go wake up my four-year-old and step in a puddle of pee from my dogs by her door since they didn't get let out at 7:00 am when they're used to being let out. I clean up the pee, wake up my nine-year-old again, and walk over to the coffee pot to turn it on just to realize I never cleaned it out from yesterday. The coffee grounds are still sitting in the filter inside the basket and the sink is filled with dirty dishes.

I move the larger dishes to the counter to create some room to wash the coffee pot and just then my daughter comes into the kitchen complaining she has nothing to wear, wants cold lunch now instead of hot lunch and to tell me the dogs pooped in her room. I mutter under my breath, "Oh, Lord, help me."

I help her find an outfit (which leads to me yelling at her and her crying), rush into the kitchen to make her cold lunch only to realize we have nothing to make because I've been meaning to go grocery shopping.

I wrestle my four-year-old daughter to get dressed and tell her to feed the dogs. As she's feeding the dogs, I change my clothes, throw my hair in a ponytail and go to grab a cup of coffee, only to realize I never made it. We were supposed to leave five minutes ago and instead of pouring the dog's food into their bowls, my daughter thought it would be funny to fill our shoes in the hallway.

I lose it on my daughter because she knows that is not the way to feed the dogs. I yell at her to get into the car and she begins to cry. I put the dogs in their room and get both girls out the door. I have no coffee, didn't brush my teeth, and forgot the "cold lunch" I completely threw together on the counter. My nine-year-old is crying because she hates being rushed and, of course, I lost it on her because she should've had her stuff picked out the night before, and she shouldn't have waited until the morning to tell me she wanted a cold lunch.

My four-year-old is also hysterical at this point because it was taking her forever to put on her shoes and to get buckled into the car, and it takes me the entire 10 minute drive to school to calm everyone down. We pull in 15 minutes late to school which triggers another meltdown for my nine-year-old because now she will miss the school breakfast and is starving. I give her a kiss and tell her everything will work out, and I promise her that I will make it up to her when she gets home.

I pull back in my driveway, go inside the house, and brew the coffee. It's Monday, so that means I have a podcast to record in front of a live audience, so with no preparation at all, I say a quick prayer that the Holy Spirit speaks on my behalf because I did not have time to prepare.

But I did have time.

I notice eight hours later there's still poop in my daughter's room that I forgot to clean up and have no idea what we're going to have for dinner tonight in one hour before we have soccer, gymnastics, and Bible study. We have no groceries because it never got done today, although it was on my to-do list. I also see all of the other things on the list that never got done: finishing my book, creating content to post for the week on social media, and getting my topic and notes picked out for my podcast recording on Wednesday.

What did *I do today?* I think to myself.

We order pizza, everyone fights over where we're getting it from. I have buyer's remorse because we're supposed to be saving money, but what am I supposed to do? We need to eat dinner. So, for the third time that week we ordered food for dinner, ate as fast as we could and began our nightly craziness of driving four kids back and forth a thousand times to activities, lessons, and practice. At 8:30 PM, I pick up the last kid, rush home and begin our nighttime routine which consists of yelling and rushing kids off to bed and handing them their iPads, hoping they just fall asleep watching it and leave me alone so that I can spend some time with my husband who I haven't seen all day.

Two hours later, I go into their rooms to take their iPads, and to my surprise, they're still awake, eyes glued to the screen. It is now midnight. I take the iPads and lay with them if they promise to go to sleep and not talk. As I fall asleep, I pray in my head for God to help my day go smoother tomorrow and to help it not be so chaotic.

At 4:00 AM, I escape back into my own room and press snooze the second my alarm goes off at 6:45 am. Nine minutes later I press snooze again and continue on the same pattern. This pattern lasts years.

Unfortunately, this pattern is one that most people find themselves in. Is it you? Are you chronically late? Find yourself triggered and snapping on your kids only to feel remorse and guilt afterwards? Always forgetting stuff? Thinking next week will be different once things die down a bit in your chaotic schedule?

What I'm describing is called reactive living. Reactive living means that something happens and then you react to it, putting out the fire or dealing with a specific situation as it pops up. The problem with this is that there are always going to be problems and things popping up, and if you're forced to deal with whatever is currently happening, you never get to prioritize the things that are really important.

This was my life until two years ago and it was hectic, chaotic, and miserable. I always felt behind, never felt like I was doing enough, and honestly felt like I was running in circles falling into bed absolutely exhausted every night but nothing was really getting done. The most important things like spending time with God and working on the projects He's called me to do like write this book and record podcast episodes to encourage women out of the valley and into their calling were always on the back burner.

Another huge thing I've been called to do—and perhaps the most important thing—is motherhood. But I wasn't thriving in that area either. I wasn't present, I wasn't in a good mood and I definitely wasn't taking good care of the blessings God had given to me.

Too Busy

Here's the thing. The devil loves when we're busy because when we're busy, we don't have time for God. If the devil can't get in front of you, he will get behind you and push you, instilling anger, fear, worry, and panic, guilt or busyness within you. He wants you distracted, feeling less than, focusing on your downfalls, and repeating over and over in your head that you're failing and not good enough.

You know what else you can't do when you're living in reactive mode? Walk the walk. You're not being a very good example to your family, not expressing the fruit of the spirit as mentioned in Galatians 5:22-23, *"But the fruit of the Spirit is love, joy, peace, patience, kindness, goodness, faithfulness, gentleness, self-control..."* These are traits you will embody the closer you become to Jesus because He will rub off on you and the Holy Spirit will shine through you so brightly, you won't even understand how it's happening. In the middle of the chaos, you will have peace and patience.

Another thing you're not doing is pouring the Word and Truth into your kids by reading the Bible, doing studies together, or just simply being available for them if they need you. When you're busy all day and don't even have time to complete the things you wrote down on your to-do list, you definitely won't have time to add anything else in there like devotionals with your kids.

See how his plan is working? Before we move on, I want to ask you this: When you get to Heaven and God asks you what you were so busy doing that you didn't know the Bible front to back, what's going to be your excuse? You were cleaning up dog pee? You were tired? You woke up late? I don't know about you, but that is not a conversation I want to be having with Our Lord God Almighty.

What we need to do is get you to start living proactively instead. It's actually a lot easier than you would think too, and even if you're a person who has never planned out your day before it starts. I'm going to teach you how because it's as simple as that.

Tip #1: Plan Tomorrow

Do not go to sleep until you have written out your tasks for the next day in the order that you will be completing them. I like to do this at the very end of my day once all my kids are in bed. I bought magnetic dry erase sheets on Amazon which came in a pack of 12 that were the perfect size for me to write out everything I had to do for the day. I like these because I can easily take them from my fridge into my office or even bring them in the car with me. Since there's 12 of them, I can stay organized and make several different lists if I need to like dinners planned for the week and to-do lists for each of my kids.

Each week, I choose 4-5 dinners we'll have that I feel like cooking, then I write them down on one of the whiteboard sheets so my family knows (and I remember). Typically, on Sundays I shop for groceries for the entire week, including all of the ingredients we need for meals. This has saved me so much time and energy because now all I have to do each night when I'm planning the next day is pick which dinner I want to make and that's it. This simple thing changed my entire life, I swear.

Tip #2: Finding The Right Planner

I utilize my calendar in my iPhone to keep track of all things that I schedule like orthodontist appointments, teeth cleanings, school functions, coaching calls, Bible studies, church events, lunch dates with friends, date nights, etc. This way, no matter where I am, I always have my phone on me, so that means I always have my calendar.

If someone asks if I can do lunch next week, I can immediately look and let them know. I also utilize the "remind" function on a lot of things like coaching calls, zooms, and meetings to go off an hour before the scheduled time so that I do not forget.

Something else I utilize alarms for is school functions. For instance, today is my four-year-old's valentine's party at her school. We signed up to bring a treat, we need valentine cards to pass out, and she also wanted a valentine's day outfit. I knew about the party back in September when she started school, and I immediately added it to my calendar but I set a "reminder" for two weeks before so I could have time to order her an outfit on Amazon and add valentine cards and treats to my shopping list, avoiding a stressful, panic-induced morning. A few weeks ago, when we signed up for specific treats, I edited the party in my calendar and wrote in the things I needed to remember to bring with me so that it would be all right there.

So, now here I am, writing my book instead of stressing out because we forgot treats, cards, and a pretty heart dress which is exactly what happened last year on Valentine's Day for my nine-year-old. You live and you learn.

If I have a wedding coming up, I set the "reminder" for a week or two ahead to have time to go to the bank and pull out money, get a card, and make sure I have a dress and my husband has a suit. See how this works?

You can use a paper planner, a digital planner, your calendar on your phone, or anything else you find that works, all we need it to do is work and accomplish this goal. I use a combination of all things now that I've found what works for me, but everyone is different, so it's very important you don't get caught up in my steps of what works for me but instead focus on you and what feels good to you. If it doesn't feel good, you're not going to do it. I tried paper planners year after year, and it just didn't work for me. I do need to physically write it down, but I need it to be displayed somewhere I see it constantly—not in a book in a drawer in my office. My mom, on the other hand, thrives with her paper planner and can't use anything else. So, find what feels good for you and your brain.

Tip #3: Displaying a Family Calendar

I have a large magnetic whiteboard calendar on my fridge for the entire month where I write out everything the family needs to know to avoid the most dreadful question I used to get on a daily basis, "What are we doing today?" Ugh, cringe. I don't know why this question is so triggering for me, maybe because when I'm asked it, I have no clue what we're doing, and it just sheds light on the fact I feel like I'm failing. Or maybe it's because they have the innate ability to ask me when I'm smack dab in the middle of chaos and meltdowns... I'm not sure, but the question HAD to stop. So now my response is, "Go check the calendar." Problem solved.

Towards the end of the month, I erase the entire calendar and write out the last few days of the month and include the entire next month. I open my calendar on my phone and first transfer everything the family needs to know onto it. As birthday parties come up, family dinners are scheduled, trips up north to visit my grandma, friends plan a sleepover, I write it on the calendar so we all know. The kids and I take turns crossing off each day as it nears its end, which is very satisfying.

Pro tip: write your calendar in a wet-erase marker. This avoids the problem of "someone" brushing up against it and erasing your precious schedule. Go get yourself a bunch of pretty colors so you can have some fun with the calendar and color code each kid or each event, however you want.

I'm going to help you get started with this because if you're going from straight chaos, you're going to need a little guidance. Maybe you're already pretty organized and put-together, in that case, you go, sis! If you want to see the exact calendars and whiteboards I use, you can visit www.tarrynsarcone.com/TheValley

Don't focus on planning out your entire month right now; just get the basics in your calendar and set all of your focus on planning tomorrow before tomorrow starts. After you get in the habit of planning one day out, then you can move to a couple of days, a week, and then a month. But for now, we're only starting with tomorrow. So, make a vow that you will not go to sleep tonight until you have your list for tomorrow.

What do you HAVE to do tomorrow? Maybe you are scheduled to work a shift, or you have appointments, kids' activities or plans, house chores, errands, dinner, etc. Whatever your plans are, write each thing down.

Once you have everything written down that you plan on accomplishing tomorrow, put them in the order that you'll do them. It's sometimes helpful for me to include the times in which I will do certain things if there are a lot, but other times, I don't need them.

Priorities

Whatever you are spending the majority of your time on are the things you are choosing to prioritize the most because you care about them the most. Sometimes this is accurate with your true priorities, while other times it's not. If you are not choosing to be proactive in your day every single day, you will automatically choose to react to it. So, if you're spending a lot of time on house chores each day and your house is spotless, but you don't have time to read your Bible, do devotions with your kids, or work on the passion projects God has laid on your heart, then there's a problem here. Of course, cleanliness and organization are important, and it shows God we're taking good care of the things He's blessed us with, but at some point we have to stop doing busy work and do the things that really hold value. You could also be wasting away your day by sleeping too much, watching too much TV, or scrolling on your phone. Ask God to open your eyes and reveal to you the areas in your life that are distracting you.

It may be helpful to make a list of the true things you value in your life and the areas in which you would like to devote the majority of your time. This exercise was extremely helpful to me when I was deep in the valley, overwhelmed, and had no clue where to even start. All I knew was that I never stopped moving throughout the day but somehow there still wasn't enough time. I would never go to bed feeling accomplished, proud, and fulfilled. Instead, I would go to bed with tremendous guilt while I lulled myself to sleep by running down the list of all the things I should've done better that day.

If you don't know your priorities, you won't be able to be proactive to them, so here's how you find out.

A professor held up a large glass jar and filled it with golf balls to the top and asked his class if they believed the jar was full. They agreed it was until he poured smaller pebbles into the jar that filled in the spaces. All the students laughed and agreed now it was full. The professor poured in sand and gently shook the jar allowing all the sand to fall in between the cracks of the pebbles. They agreed that now it was full. The last thing he did was pour some water into it and now it was completely full. But he asked if everything would fit into this jar if you did it the other way around, and of course, that answer is no. If you started with the water, nothing else would fit in without the water overflowing.

This jar is your life. If you don't add in the biggest most important things to your jar first, you won't have room for them at all. So, your golf balls are your biggest priorities and the things that matter most to you. My golf balls are my kids, my husband, running my house, my personal time with God, my close friends, my health, church, ministry, writing, and my podcast. These are the things that come before anything else, and I plan them and strategically place them in the jar first. This means that everything else comes after, like meeting a new friend for coffee, deep cleaning my house, taking on extra projects, saying yes to other ministries/projects ... You get the picture. You should have about 8-10 golf balls, so take a minute in your journal and write down what they are, or just pause this and make yourself a little note to remember to do this later on.

After you do this and see your golf balls, take some time and schedule them into your calendar one by one so that you can begin living a proactive life. Don't skip this step and continue to live your life in reaction mode. This book will only work if you do the steps.

"Look carefully then how you walk, not as unwise but as wise, making the best use of the time, because the days are evil. Therefore, do not be foolish, but understand what the will of the Lord is" (Ephesians 5:15-17).

ENERGY LEAKS

Let's start out by defining an energy leak. Since I'm a mother of four, let's use the example of a refrigerator door being left open all night long. What would happen to the food inside? It would spoil because the energy from the refrigerator would be escaping out the door—this is an energy leak. The refrigerator is you—your soul, your well-being, your mindset, your attitude, etc. The door being left open are the things in your life that are wreaking havoc in the back of your mind, causing all of your focus and energy to spill out. The longer you ignore the refrigerator door being open, the more spoiled the food becomes.

Let me give you some examples of real energy leaks in my life.

My largest energy leak is a messy, unorganized house and work space. There is no way that I can sit down and focus on something like writing this book, creating content for social media, or planning an event if my house is in utter chaos. A sink full of dishes, clothes and toys everywhere, laundry backed up, dog hair blowing across my hardwood floors, random snack bowls left all around my house, and every couch pillow on the floor causes my mind to literally shut down. And forget about diving into a deep focus session if my office is a mess with Barbies and baby dolls everywhere, thanks to my four-year-old who's obsessed with playing there. Bills and papers are everywhere, books are out, and little hole punch circles from my nine-year-old are covering the floor. This is causing my energy to leak out at a very fast pace.

Scientifically, this can be proven since objects take up space which take up energy. A study in the US in 2008 found that mothers who lived within a messy, unorganized home had way higher cortisol levels (stress hormones) than mothers who didn't. This also can affect anxiety levels and sleep since the visual distractions of clutter increase cognitive overload. I have also found that the clutter, mess, or disorganization influences other areas of our life as well like our emotions, behavior, and relationships with others.

I'm not saying that your house needs to be completely clean and perfect in order to get any work done, but you cannot neglect it entirely and be able to dive into your best work. You'll be surprised at what 15 minutes of power cleaning can actually do for your house and your energy.

Before I go any further, it's important to mention that we do not want to get stuck in a cycle of extreme preparation and perfection before we dive in and begin something. So many of us use this as an excuse to never even begin the project in the first place. There is always something more to do. Your brain will come up with a never-ending list of things to do before you begin a project, especially if surrounding the project is any fear, insecurity, or doubt. Typically, when God gives us a big vision or dream or speaks into our lives, it's always far greater than what we see ourselves achieving, and we tend to feel unequipped. In those circumstances, even cleaning a bathroom sounds more enjoyable than working on a book, launching your podcast, recording the course or more. So do not get stuck here. Write down "Done Beats Perfect" on a sticky note if you struggle with perfection like I do, and read it over and over to yourself.

Aside from a messy house, a common energy leak I find most women have in common is this never-ending to-do list in the back of our brains of things that need to get done "one day." These things include cleaning out the junk drawer, organizing the cabinets, cleaning out old clothes that no longer fit us or the kids, getting old toys together to donate, connecting with old friends, cleaning out the attic, and the list goes on and on. None of these things are urgent and need to be done right now, but they're nagging us every time we see them, causing our inner voice to repeat, "There's another thing you haven't done yet." (As if we're not hard enough on ourselves already.)

Other things that are depleting our energy include unresolved conflict with someone in our lives, unforgiveness, bitterness, resentment, or poor boundaries. If something (or someone) is triggering you, that also will drain you (more on triggers in chapter 17). Even things like addiction, whether it be your own or a friend/family member, will be the cause of draining your energy very quickly.

There's a lot that's happening in your circle that we need to first become aware of and then work to fix by giving it to God and asking for His help. You can't do this alone. Add a prayer in your journal asking God for discernment and wisdom to see the areas of your life that are draining your energy.

Brain Dump

Set a timer on your phone for 15 minutes and make a list of every single thing that is being held in your brain that you know you need to do. Everyone you need to call, appointments you've been avoiding making for some reason, bills you need to pay, work you need to get done, everything.

It may be helpful to run through some categories in your life to help jog your memory. Categories I use are: church, family, friends, health, finances, career. We're calling this a brain dump because you are dumping everything out of your brain that doesn't need to be there and making one big huge master list of everything. Don't worry about organizing it or thinking too much about each task, just write it down and get it out of your brain. Pause this book and do this right now, I promise you it's going to feel so good.

Sometimes when I have a ton on my to-do list and I'm feeling overwhelmed, I'll start by putting a star next to all the tasks that take 10 minutes or less and work through those things first. Or you probably have some things that are more urgent than others and have deadlines. If this is the case, work by most important to least important. If you just flat out don't feel like doing any of it, then I suggest the tennis shoe trick.

Tennis Shoe Trick

Tony Robbins says in order to change your mental state you must first change your physical state. I have used this trick for years and I would be lying if I said I made it up. My Mom is the one who taught me this trick. First start off by putting on your favorite, most comfortable pair of tennis shoes, get into a comfortable cleaning outfit, put your hair up, open all the blinds, turn on some music and set a timer for 15 minutes. During this time, I try to move as quickly as possible and also make sure that all of my kids know before I begin that I have these 15 minutes blocked in my day, so I will not stop to help with anything. This is called setting boundaries, and it took me many, many years to learn.

During this 15-minute time frame, start doing anything on your list that you feel like doing. A lot of times I'm not feeling creative, I'm isolating and ignoring my inbox, but dead-heading and watering my flowers sounds wonderful. Or all of a sudden, I'm in the mood to vacuum the couch or clean out the junk drawer. Just start doing something! Anything at all that's on the list.

Setting Up For Success

Once you have everything written down on your master to-do list, you need to schedule the time to take care of all of these things. My favorite thing to do is to schedule out an entire weekend where all I do is work on things from this list. That may or may not work for you. Maybe you only have an hour in your schedule each day to work on this list for the week or a few hours each morning. Figure out what's going to work for you realistically. If you haven't had any time to get anything done lately, don't write out 10 things from this master list to do tomorrow. You're only setting yourself up to fail.

The worst time in my house where it is the most chaotic is between 4pm-9pm. Everyone wants a snack, everyone wants to tell me about their day, everyone has stuff to get done before evening activities, dinner, showers, and preparing for the next day. It is insane. I never schedule anything from the hours of 4pm-9pm because of it. My focus is 100% on my family during those times so it would be awful, stressful, and more draining of my energy to try to do it in that time frame.

During this block of time that you are chipping away at the list, you should try to fill your brain with as much positivity as possible. If you're doing a mindless task like folding laundry, driving kids around, or going through junk drawers, you can multitask by listening to a sermon, favorite podcaster, or an audio book. While you're cleaning up energy leaks you're also clearing up the negativity in your brain and allowing your brain to focus on someone else talking instead of listening to itself talk and spew negativity.

You cannot get out of the valley if you ignore this step on Energy Leaks.

Easy as 1...2...3...

When I sense myself going back into the valley, there are three things I do to get out of it that work every single time. It's a 3-step technique I teach people who want to get their life back on track right now. The first thing I tell them to do is to take control of your mind and shut your brain off (as we discussed in chapter nine).

The second step is to switch from reactive living to proactive living, discussed in chapter ten.

The third step is to patch up your energy leaks (which were discussed in this chapter).

It really is as simple as 1, 2, 3.

When you do this, your brain relaxes, you start to feel accomplished, you have hope things won't always be this way, and you see a light at the end of the tunnel.

The real trick is staying out of the valley once you get out. As you do this and re-read the chapters in this book over and over again, you will get better and better at these techniques and will start living so proactively that you never even get energy leaks in your life because you deal with them way before they become an energy leak. For example, as I mentioned previously, on the weekends I get groceries for the week ahead, plan out all my dinners, check our schedule, write down any errands I need to run, projects I need to complete, and tasks at work I need to focus on. This avoids me feeling overwhelmed and unprepared during the week, causing an energy leak. Another thing I do to help avoid energy leaks is to pick up my house before bed, and make sure I stay on top of the kids before bed to do their chores like dishes or laundry so it's not all on me.

I know this isn't a parenting book, but if you have children and they're not doing chores and helping you around the house, please get them started with this. Everyone lives there, everyone can work together, and this shouldn't be all on you. If everything is on you to do, that is draining and exhausting, no matter how much planning and preparation you do. Even young children can complete tasks. Check on Pintrest for a creative list of ideas.

Each of my kids has a magnetic whiteboard on the fridge with their name on it. I will add things to their to-do list from my to-do list that I think they could help with. By writing it down, I don't need to remember what I told them to do and I don't need to remind them over and over again. They now know that they need to check their to-do lists first thing in the morning, and they have to have my stuff done before they do any of their own things. It took a little while to implement this, but after a few days, they stopped complaining (as much) and started helping. I make sure to tell them what a huge help they've been to me, how much I appreciate them, and how important they are to me.

Remember that energy is constantly flowing, which means it's constantly changing. If you are feeling overwhelmed, stressed, worried, doubtful, and you're over-analyzing, you're over-thinking, you are starting to panic and anxiety is creeping in, remember that "this too shall pass." It's not forever and you can change the way you feel faster than you'd ever imagine. All you have to remember is the 3 steps outlined in chapters 9, 10, and 11. These will be the most-read chapters in this book because you will have to come back here often to remind yourself how to get out.

Going into a valley isn't something you should fear. Valleys are common and will happen over and over again, and a lot of times the tension we feel in the valley is what teaches us our greatest lessons in life. It's getting out of the valley that you should focus on. By applying these last three chapters to your life and using them as a guide, you will be able to get out of the valley within a few days instead of it taking years, months, or even weeks.

CHAPTER 12

THERAPY

When I was working in the sales and marketing world, I hit a plateau and it felt like no matter what I did, how hard I worked, or how much I sacrificed, I could not grow past the level I was at. I knew there was something holding me back, and I knew intuitively that it had something to with abandonment issues from my biological father. All I wanted to do was find out what it was so that I could be on my way to making millions of dollars and achieving the worldly success my heart was after.

I've been to see a therapist a few times in my life, only to last a couple of sessions and then stop going because I either didn't mesh well with the therapist, felt I no longer needed help or just simply felt I was too busy or too broken to continue my sessions.

So maybe you've tried to talk with someone before, or maybe you believe the lie that you just need to suck it up and get over it. Life is hard. Either way, I'm begging you to pray for God to lead you to the right professional to talk to that will help you to heal past wounds and learn about why you are the way that you are. Please make sure the person you see is a Christian because it makes all the difference; this is crucial.

In 2020, I promised myself I would go to therapy for an entire year straight or as many times as my therapist wanted me to. I started out going twice a week, then went down to once a week, every other week, and then once a month for the last two months out of the year. It's ironic, because I started going to grow in my business and I ended up walking away from it entirely.

I learned more in therapy about myself that year than I have in any way all the years I've been alive combined. One thing I learned was that I am a verbal processor, so simply talking about how I feel makes me feel better, have more clarity, and be able to feel sane and heard.

A lot of us are verbal processors, but we don't have anybody to talk to who understands us, knows the right questions to ask us, and is supportive and encouraging throughout the entire process. For example, I would have all the "valley feels" and desperately need to talk about it with someone so I would talk with my husband after the kids went to bed. I'd pour my heart out to him, cry, and tell him how alone I truly felt in my life. Although my husband is a good man, a godly man, and would do anything for me, he heard my message as I'm not happy and he took ownership in that a little as I'm his wife, and he wants me to be happy. So instead of hearing me and understanding, he felt attacked, couldn't fix the problem, and that left me feeling more alone and hurt. He just didn't understand how I was feeling especially because he has never struggled with his mental health a day in his life and just "gets over it", which I am so envious of.

The people in our lives want to help us and want to be there for us but just don't know how. Professionals have a passion to help, are educated in how to help, and have this amazing way of making you feel sane, like no matter what you're thinking or doing they've seen or heard it all before.

When I walked into my therapist's office and sat in the big maroon winged-back chair facing an identical one she was sitting in, I told her I was there to "get over whatever it was with my dad that was holding back from achieving more in life" but, when she began asking me questions about my dad and my life, I began to sob uncontrollably. I couldn't even talk about it. This is how I knew it was holding me back. I've learned that if something touches you so deeply and emotionally, it's because it has some sort of soul tie to you and truly matters to you.

Transitioning

Another helpful thing I learned in therapy was that I have a lot of difficulty transitioning between activities and shifting my focus quickly from one thing to the next, and this was the cause of my mood swings and my random bad attitudes towards my kids and husband. I couldn't figure out why all of a sudden, I would have a drastic change in my mood. One minute I'm working and coaching someone, feeling amazing and on fire for God and my purpose, and the next minute I was in the worst mood when my kids arrived home from school or my husband showed up at the front door from work. I was thrilled they were home, I missed them and loved them, but my actions didn't prove that. It was affecting my marriage because my husband felt he had to walk on eggshells around me guessing which kind of mood I would be in. It also made me have this tremendous amount of mom guilt for treating my kids the way I was.

The reason I'm mentioning transitions is because most people struggle with this and have no clue, so I'm hoping to shed a little light on the topic in this chapter. If you think you may struggle with transitioning, here are some things you're going to want to add in between blocks of time. I used to work right up until 4pm when my boys would get home off the bus from school. I would be on an important coaching call from 3pm-4pm and it would end up running a few minutes over, they would be standing in the kitchen waiting for me to get off the phone and then I would hang up and instantly go from Life Coach to Mom.

I would be pulled in two different directions by each boy wanting to show me what they did in school, tell me stories of things that happened, ask questions about the evening, and help with homework. I also needed to start dinner and usually had no clue what I was going to make, and we didn't even have groceries. So, this would trigger a breakdown that would come out in a bad mood towards my kids. I would be irritated with them talking to me because my brain would be on thinking about dinner and groceries and how much we had in the budget to spend on food tonight. I would be irritated with them for no reason at all, just simply being kids and being excited to share part of their world with their mom.

So, here's what I learned to do in between during the transition period. I would leave about 30 minutes to an hour to transition and would do things like nap, read a book, clean up my house, start cooking, take a shower and get ready, work out, go for a walk outside, stretch, pray, journal, do a devotional, study my Bible, or change my clothes.

It is mind-blowing how well all of these things work for someone who struggles transitioning. It's also important you let your family know you struggle with this so they can give you the space you need and the time to transition.

You're Normal

Another benefit of therapy is to learn why you are the way that you are. It's comforting to know that you act exactly like the person who experienced what you experienced would act. You're not crazy, you're not totally broken or damaged. You have experienced things in your life that have made you into who you are today.

For example, I felt abandoned by my father, so I developed personality traits because of that like control (to protect me from ever being abandoned and hurt again) and the need for approval from others. A professional will help you to dive deep into your emotions and past wounds, which, let me be honest, sucks while you're doing it and feels awful, but it works. Most of us brush problems under the rug by never dealing with what happened, and all that does is cause other problems later on in life. You have to talk about it in order to understand it and then to heal from it.

The goal in therapy for me was to heal my past wounds, forgive my dad, make amends with him, and then reconcile our relationship. I did not want to do any of this, after all, I did repeat over and over again in my mind how much I didn't care that my dad wasn't in my life, but I actually cared so much. When you can truly forgive, make amends in your heart, and then reconcile with the people who have wronged you, abused you or abandoned you, you begin to experience true freedom in Christ. Our own flesh doesn't want to forgive, doesn't want to heal and move on, we want to get even. We want revenge.

But God talks about revenge a lot in the Bible, and here's what He has to say about it: Proverbs 24:29 says, *"Do not say, 'I will do to him as he has done to me; I will pay the man back for what he has done.'"* In Romans 12:19, He says, *"Beloved, never avenge yourselves, but leave it* to the wrath of God, for it is written, 'Vengeance is mine, I will repay, says the Lord.'"

Aside from vengeance, the scripture is extremely clear on forgiving others. Matthew 6:15 says, *"But if you do not forgive others their trespasses, neither will your Father forgive your trespasses."* Proverbs 10:12 says, *"Hatred stirs up strife, but love covers all offenses."*

Of course, the devil would want you seeing red in rage and anger, causing even more hatred in the world. But by giving your past to God and asking Him for understanding, healing, and to see the situation through His eyes, you will start to gain a whole lot of clarity of your life in a whole different way.

I went from hating my father and not even being able to talk about him at all without crying to having this deep compassionate love for him. Through therapy and God opening my eyes by removing the scales and softening my heart, I started to see my father as God did. He did the best he could with what he had. He was a teenager when he had me, had a lot of generational sin and struggles himself, and was trying to just get by and do the right thing the best way he could.

My point is that Jesus changed my heart and my entire mindset and I finally got to a point just a few months into therapy that I needed to see and talk with my dad, I needed to forgive him and make amends. It was such a strong feeling from the Holy Spirit to do this because my flesh was completely against it from the beginning. Even though I didn't want to, my body did, and I went forward with contacting him and scheduling a time for me and him to connect in person.

Driving to his house to see him, there was not one nervous fiber in my body. I was completely calm and at peace, not even nervous to see him for the first time in several years. This is how I knew this was God because I had peace that surpassed all understanding as he says you will get in Philippians 4:6, *"Do not be anxious about anything. Instead, in every situation with prayer and petition with thanksgiving, tell your requests to God. And the peace that surpasses all understanding will guard your hearts and minds in Christ Jesus."*

When I connected in person with my dad, I immediately knew God had bigger plans and that He was using me to share Jesus with Him. My dad desperately needed a savior, healing, and comfort. To think that I was so filled with hatred and offense that I would've kept him from knowing that peace and comfort. I realized right then and there that it wasn't all about me. I knew the exact reason why I felt so strongly in my soul to go to therapy and heal my relationship with my dad because the Holy Spirit knew I was one of the only people whom he would listen to.

During this conversation with him, I realized all I truly wanted to do in my life was to coach others and help them improve their own life. I was no longer interested in sales and marketing and making money. I was interested in helping people improve their lives with Jesus, starting with my dad.

Therapy also taught me that the reason I wanted to succeed in life so badly was because I wanted the approval of others. I learned throughout my life that if I had money, people would like me, so I thought the more I made, the more I would be liked, and the better I would feel. But with more money never came more satisfaction and more true authentic friends. It was as if the higher I climbed, the more alone I actually felt. So, although I started therapy to get a raise and achieve new ranks throughout my company, I realized that it wasn't really what I was after. I really wanted to be satisfied, joyful, and abundant—all things I could only ever achieve by connecting intimately with Jesus.

So please, be in prayer about finding a Christian professional who will help you dive into your past, figure out why you act the way you act, and break free from all that is holding you back. There is no shame in getting help. If you can't do it for yourself, do it for your future generations to come. If you're angry and don't know why, it's time you learn why. If you've been disloyal in your marriage, it's time to learn why and heal. If you struggle with not feeling worthy or you let fear completely take over, it's time to learn why and stop the cycle once and for all. You can get past this, you can heal, and you can become who you want to be–who you were created to be in Christ.

Journal prompt: Grab your journal and write this question down followed by your answer.

Question: What are some things I want to stick with during the next year to help with my growth and healing?

I had you write out the journal prompt of what you want to stick with over the next year because that's the minimum amount of time we're going to give ourselves to heal and grow out of the valley for good. It's taken you 20, 30, 50, or even 60 years to get this far down into the valley. You have to give yourself grace and a realistic timeframe to get out, and I don't think a year is too much to ask.

FOLLOW HIM

If you want to continue to grow out of the valley and towards the peak of abundance, joy and fulfillment, you need to make sure you continue to follow Jesus every single day. As the mountain gets a bit steeper towards the top, one wrong step and you could slide all the way back down. This is why we need to be constantly focused on Jesus ahead of us and the path He has already created for us by laying out breadcrumbs for us to follow. The next chapter is dedicated entirely to breadcrumbs, so don't get too caught up on that right now.

I want you to imagine that you're walking through the woods. It's a beautiful fall day and there are different colored leaves all over the ground, stained in beautiful shades of red, orange, and yellow. They crunch beneath your feet as you walk over them, following behind Jesus. It's sunny, the air is fresh, and the path is nicely groomed. Jesus is within an arm's length away from you, so He's easy to follow (at first). This is what it's like the moment you accept Christ into your life and decide you will follow Him. It seems easy, simple, and you are confident you will be following him intently daily for the rest of your life. But then life happens, you get distracted, you forget to follow as closely as you were. You're too busy to read your Bible, you're too busy to get deep in prayer, your life gets the best of you, throwing things your way so the only thing you feel you have time for is reacting and diving out of the way. You're putting out fires everywhere you go. Forget living... Because at this point, you are only trying to survive.

But what happened? How does someone go from feeling like they are on top of the world—free, abundant, chosen, and special to feeling suffocated, imprisoned, abandoned, forgotten, and not enough all within a couple of days or hours?

It's because we stop following and resume normal life. We must learn what it means to follow Christ every single day. This is the most important instruction in this book. If you don't remember anything from this besides this chapter, I will be grateful because none of the other chapters matter if you do not follow Him daily.

To truly follow Christ means He has become everything to you. In Exodus 20:3, Jesus says, *"You shall have no other gods before me."* It's easy for us to think of "gods" as big powerful booming figures from the sky, but truly "gods" can be anything we serve and focus on. For me, I worshiped money and success like gods; they were my idols as previously mentioned. I followed them every single day. The second I woke up, it was the first thing on my mind and the last when I finally went to bed.

You can tell what someone worships by their calendar. I was not following Jesus in that season of my life, although I definitely considered myself a Christian at that time. I believed in everything Jesus had done for me, went to church most Sundays, and prayed occasionally. If I would've died right then at that moment, I would've gone to Heaven, but I wouldn't have taken many people with me. I was not following Jesus, and that is why life was so hard for me. I felt alone, isolated, worried, doubtful, depressed, anxious, and lost. When I started following Jesus and reading His words by waking up with Him every single morning, it was no wonder I had felt so miserable. The scripture outlines it all.

Scriptures like John 8:12 when Jesus says, *"I am the light of the world. Whoever follows me will not walk in darkness, but will have the light of life."* That is why I felt alone and confused because I was walking down a dark path trying to find my own way.

For a while I tricked myself into thinking that I was following Jesus and success together, making sure I was putting Jesus first, but then I read *"No one can serve two masters, for either he will hate the one and love the other, or he will be devoted to the one and despise the other. You cannot serve God and money"* (Matthew 6:24).

Was this really in the Bible?! I couldn't believe it.

Maybe it's not money that you've followed and worshiped. Maybe it's approval of others, friendships, culture or selfish desires. But just remember, whatever it is, you cannot serve it and God at the same time. To truly follow Christ means we do not follow anything else. I have found this to be extremely hard to do on my own, actually I would even say it's impossible to do it on our own. Your willpower simply isn't enough to follow Jesus daily. We are so weak in our own flesh, that is why we need the Holy Spirit to work through us, to renew us and lead us. In John 6:63, Jesus says, *"For it is the Spirit who gives us life; the flesh is no hope at all..."*

Jesus also talks about the Holy Spirit in John 14:15-17 by saying, *"If you love me, you will keep my commandments. And I will ask the Father, and he will give you another Helper, to be with you forever, even the Spirit of truth, whom the world cannot receive, because it neither sees him nor knows him. You know him, for he dwells with you and will be in you."*

Jesus promised many times throughout his ministry on earth that, once He had ascended to the Father, He would send a "Helper" to them—the Holy Spirit. John 14:26 is a perfect example of this, Jesus said, *"But the Helper, the Holy Spirit, whom the Father will send in my name, he will teach you all things and bring to your remembrance all that I have said."* Jesus told them that it was for their own good that He was going away so that the Spirit could come indwell the heart of every believer. So, because He died on the cross, the Holy Spirit has been available to anyone who believes.

Following Jesus means striving to be like Him every single day. He always obeyed His Father, so that's what we strive to do. To truly follow Christ means to make Him the Lord of our life, and that means completely submitting to His will for us.

The good news is that the Spirit does it for us, so we don't have to strive in our own flesh by hustling, plotting, planning, and scheming. Instead, connect to God first every single day and ask Him what His will is for our life. He is the boss of our life, so without connecting to Him and listening to the instructions for your assignment that day, you'll have no idea what to do and begin doing things the way you believe them to be done—in the flesh.

To follow Christ means we learn the truths he spoke about in the Bible and then apply them in our lives. The more we do this, the more we become like Jesus, expressing the fruit of the spirit.

For me, distractions have been the number one reason I have lost sight of Jesus. It's not because I don't believe in His word or believe in my assignment, but because I simply forget what's important. I wake up and immediately go into mom mode, focusing on everyone and everything else—the house, the chores, and then my own job, dinner, driving kids around to after school activities. Then start the bedtime routine with my littles and off to bed I go, absolutely so exhausted, praying to God tomorrow will be different.

Proactive living is a great way to make sure that your time with God is prioritized and therefore is happening. For me, the only thing that has helped me to wake up and instantly set my mind on things above instead of earthly things is to have some sort of accountability and someplace to be. That is how my WAKE UP! With Tarryn Sarcone podcast came about. I would get a few soul sisters together on Zoom first thing in the morning and give them a pep talk (but secretly I was pep-talking myself the most) on where God wants us to focus on that day. I would read scripture, tell everyone what I had been learning, sermons I'd been listening to, and we would just talk about our own lives and where we saw God working.

I finally started having some sort of structure to the calls and I would prepare topics in advance. I opened the calls up to anyone who wanted to join and would record for those who couldn't make it on with us at the time we were gathering. I started posting the recordings on YouTube and then just the audio files onto a podcast platform. The more episodes I recorded, I felt the Holy Spirit speaking through me and I started letting go of my topics and structure and allowing the Holy Spirit to move through me and His people. The result was mind-blowing. More and more unfulfilled Christian women began listening to the podcast, and now as I write this, we have over 18k listeners.

This tells me how many women need to wake up and set their minds on Christ. Even for those listening to the recordings, I strongly advise that they're listened to first thing in the morning to set your intentions on things that truly matter. So, while you're getting ready, driving into work or driving to drop your kids at school, running errands or doing chores, you can pop in an ear bud and listen to an episode to start your day.

I have to wake up every day and do this. When I first started doing this, I would listen to old episodes of my podcast or choose a Christian audio book to listen to. After a while, I realized the importance of spending time with God just 1-on-1 first thing in the morning.

At first, I didn't know how to do this, and the Bible was so intimidating that listening to things really helped me to get through. But I want to strongly advise you that although it's a great place to start, and my podcast or other Christian books and sermons are excellent tools, you can't only rely on this.

You need to create space to sit down and talk with God 1-on-1—praying, reading scripture, reading through the Bible, journaling, or simply sitting and listening to what God will download in your mind. This is like doing anything for the first time. At first, it feels awkward, you're not very good at it, not sure if you're doing it right, and don't quite understand everything about it. But the more you practice, the more you show up, the more you try and learn about God, the better you will be at this. All God wants is to spend time with us. He doesn't need our perfection, He wants our true, authentic selves admitting we can't do this alone and meeting with Him daily for guidance and instruction.

The Bible is filled with scriptures of God expressing this to us. First Peter 2:2 says, *"Like newborn infants, long for the pure spiritual milk, that by it you may grow up into salvation."* James 4:8 says, *"Draw near to God, and he will draw near to you."* First Chronicles 16:11 says, *"Seek the Lord and his strength; seek his presence continually!"*

On days when I don't do this, usually because I tell myself I don't have time or I am too tired to wake up any earlier because I stayed up too late and wasn't proactive about my day (I STILL fall off the wagon sometimes too), my entire day is thrown off. I find myself irritated, over-thinking, worrying, doubting and stressing about everything. Not to mention my mood is directly impacted by this, having a shorter-than-normal fuse with my kids. I'm angry for no reason and just feeling burnt out and exhausted, like I'm too weak to deal with everything that comes my way. And it's exactly what scripture says will happen when we try to do life on our own. In Matthew 11:29, Jesus says, *"Take my yoke upon you and learn from me, for I am gentle and lowly in heart, and you will find rest for your souls."* To understand this scripture, it's crucial you understand what "take my yoke upon you" means. A yoke is a wooden cross piece that is fastened over the necks of two animals and attached to the plow or cart that they are to pull. The purpose of the yoke is to connect two animals together, allowing the stronger one to set the pace and do more work than the weaker animal. This ensures the weaker animal doesn't fall behind, and so that it doesn't get burnt out faster than the other.

The scripture in Matthew 11:29 is telling us to connect ourselves to God, in his word, in his ways, and in his instruction so that life is a bit easier for us. When we do this, we don't get burnt out so quickly and feel like we're carrying the load alone. We're not alone, no matter what we do, and God does not leave us. But if you take off the yoke and try to do the work on your own, you're going to burn out.

So, whatever you do, make sure you show up for your appointment with God every day. It doesn't have to be perfect, but it does have to be consistent. I guarantee if you woke up for the next three days and spent at least 30 minutes with God, you would have a life-changing experience. Start out by proactively scheduling your appointment with God into your schedule for tomorrow and make a list right now of at least 5 things you want to talk to Him about.

For a complete list of my favorite books, devotions, Bible studies, and sermons for someone who is in the valley and trying to get out, visit **www.tarrynsarcone.com/TheValley**

BREADCRUMBS

Ever since I was a little girl, I loved mushroom hunting with my Grandmother up north. She lived basically in the middle of the woods on a dead-end dirt road surrounded by pine trees, ferns, and two-track roads. During a specific season, when the mushrooms would be popping up, we would head out with a plastic grocery bag and we would begin our hunt.

I don't know if you've ever hunted for a mushroom, but it can be a lot harder than it sounds. Most mushrooms grow underneath leaves and ferns, making it almost impossible to notice without moving your hand close to the soil. Also, the mushrooms we were looking for were camouflaged, making it even harder to spot. We would have to walk slowly and intentionally stare at the ground, for if you got distracted for even a couple of minutes looking at something else, you could miss a whole bunch of them all in one spot.

Hunting for mushrooms is a lot like following Jesus. If you get distracted while following Him and start looking around, you'll miss the next clue He has laid out for you to follow telling you which way to go next.

I'm not sure if God automatically lays breadcrumbs for us down our path or if we have to ask for it to be done for us. But I do know that if you are not asking, I promise you are also not looking for them. So, if you want to start noticing the breadcrumbs, then it is extremely important you spend some time with God 1-on-1, asking Him to lead you to your next breadcrumb.

One way I do this is by praying: "Light the path or slam the door." I need Him to illuminate the breadcrumbs for me so that I don't miss them and I can see clear as day where the path leads. I like to do this first thing in the morning. I pray for Him to bring me people who are missing pieces to this puzzle, people who are meant to connect with me for whatever reason. I pray that God guides me to my next lesson I need to learn, the next book I need to read, or the person I need to meet.

Then, I listen and watch. This is the hardest thing for me to do, believe it or not. When I first started doing this, it seemed impossible to just be still. But the more I learned about God's ways, the more I saw how much hustle, plotting, and scheming didn't really matter. If it's not God's will for your life, no matter how hard you try, you will never make it happen.

Also, another thing I tried doing was trying to run ahead of Jesus on the path and show Him which way we should go. Wrong move. I think it's because of the world and culture we live in today why everyone is so fast-paced, or all of our advancing technology, robots, and apps that help us get our tasks done quicker and more effectively, but it's really hard for people to be patient these days.

The thing I learned about being impatient is that it's pretty much the same thing as not trusting in God. If you truly believe that He is in control, that He is the way, the truth, and the life, then you will eventually learn to submit to His ways, which also include His timing.

Do you know what the Bible says about being still? Psalm 46:10 says, *"Be still, and know that I am God."* In Exodus 14:14, we hear another powerful scripture from Moses that says, *"The Lord will fight for you, and you have only to be silent."* He gave these instructions to the Israelites right after they left Egypt as slaves and began their journey into the Promised Land but saw Pharaoh and his massive army coming for them! Moses says right before that scripture to not be afraid and to stand firm.

Are you afraid? Are you letting fear control you? Get behind you and push you? Or get in front of you and freeze you? Emotions like fear, worry, and doubt are distractions that will keep you from finding your next breadcrumb, so don't let them take over your mind. If you're having a hard time with your mind racing and it feels completely out of your control? Go back and reread chapter 9: Rewire/Reprogram your brain.

Praying for breadcrumbs is the first step, however, it goes along with step two, which is moving towards them. If you notice all the breadcrumbs laid before you but you do absolutely nothing with them, nothing will happen, and you won't move forward down the path. It takes two legs to walk, so one leg is noticing the breadcrumbs and the other is doing something about them.

Have you been hearing about the same topic lately everywhere you go? You turn on the radio and they're talking about it, the scripture read during Sunday service is about it, your daily devotion you pick up is about it, and heck, even your small group is talking about it. There's a pretty good chance that this topic is a breadcrumb for you and God really wants to make sure you're listening, learning, and understanding the topic fully.

Has someone recommended a book to you out of the blue, and the second you hear about it you have a quickness in your breath and you know without a doubt you need to read it? Breadcrumb.

You have a hunch that you should sit at a certain table during the women's event at your church, so you sit down and end up meeting someone who seems to be the perfect fit in your puzzle. Breadcrumb.

A breadcrumb is more than instructions or advice from someone, it's a feeling you get when you notice the breadcrumb. You have to tap into your intuition and connect with The Holy Spirit and pray that the Spirit helps you to notice the breadcrumbs. I get daily recommendations on books to read. It's rare, but sometimes the title or blurb hits me right in the soul. I just know I have to stop everything and download it. Breadcrumb!

This past summer, I was invited to attend a women's retreat with a group of 40 women from my church and about 250 from surrounding churches. We would be heading up into Northern Michigan during the beautiful month of August. I love the end of summer in Michigan, I love camping, I love retreats, and I love getaways, but I also have this annoying anxiety that creeps up when traveling is mentioned without my Husband.

The moment the words came out of my friend's mouth inviting me to the retreat, I knew in the deepest part of my soul I had to go but because of my anxiety I procrastinated signing up. I didn't know too many people. Who would I share a room with? Who would I drive there with? Who would I sit with? What would the speaker be like? What would the weekend theme be? How much free time would we have? And the questions went on and on in my mind, over-analyzing every single thought.

If you're a type A personality like me, you like to be in control, have a plan, and be prepared. But I spent time in prayer asking God what He wanted me to do, and I couldn't shake the feeling in my gut that I needed to go, so I reluctantly said, "Yes."

So, I fill up my car with women and we head north, arrive, unpack our bags, and head to our first session where we all meet the speaker for the first time. Melissa Spoelstra gets on stage and introduces herself and says she's a published Christian author. I look at my friend Summer, who I was sitting next to, and I tell her that I know the reason I needed to come to the retreat was to connect with Melissa. God had been telling me to write a book for the last year but I had no idea where to even begin. My book was all I could think about and obsess over. I knew that God wanted me to write it, I knew that the message I would share would help so many women get out of the valley and into their calling, but I had no idea where to begin. I felt overwhelmed, unequipped, and lost.

I broke out in tears in the audience, feeling the love God had for me. Knowing that He was leading and guiding me down this path and how capable He thought I was. I was so happy I decided to let go of the fear, unknown, and control and say yes to the event anyway.

During her first teaching session I wrote in my journal how I couldn't wait to see what God had planned for me. I wrote the letters "BC" and circled them next to it. This is a code I've used for years to identify breadcrumbs in my life that I journal about. Most of the time, I can identify a breadcrumb right away when I journal about it for the first time, but once in a while I'll have to go back and identify things I journal about that in hindsight I can see were crumbs.

Journaling breadcrumbs is crucial in your journey with God out of the valley and into your calling for several reasons. The biggest reason is so that you don't forget them and you are able to look back and see God's hand on your life this entire time. Secondly, it helps you to build confidence and trust with God, seeing Him show up and guide you day after day knowing that He will never leave you hanging. He will never abandon you on the path and He will never change His mind about you. He's crazy about you and wants you to continue taking steps towards your calling. Don't ever let the devil get into your head and tell you otherwise because he's gonna try. Trust me.

Journaling breadcrumbs is so helpful because it allows you to go back and reread your entries in a different emotion. In chapter 9, we learned about emotional lenses and how when you're in a certain emotional state, it's hard (actually impossible) to see the big picture clearly. Journaling and then going back through to read it will help you get a clearer picture of what God's doing in and through you. This also has helped me tremendously build my confidence in the fact that I can hear from God and that I need to stop doubting or down-playing that ability.

After Melissa got off the stage, I was one of the first people with all of my belongings packed up and headed out the back doors to meet her. I walked over to her table where she was selling her own books—mostly devotionals and Bible studies—and said, "Hi. My name is Tarryn and I'm writing a book, and for whatever reason, God wanted me to come introduce myself to you. So, here I am... Do you have any pointers for me?" She asked about my book and then told me that she had just posted that day on her social media that she was taking applications for interns that following year and she told me that I should apply. I thanked her and told her I would and went back to my room. I pulled out my journal and wrote that I knew the entire reason why I was to be at this retreat was to become an intern for Melissa Spoelstra. I already knew the position was mine.

Fast forward a couple of months. I get an email congratulating me that I have received the design internship position with Melissa and in turn will be coached by her in the areas of writing and speaking—everything that I have been interested in.

I have so many examples of breadcrumbs I could go on for hours. At first, I didn't recognize them at all, but as I practiced praying in the morning for guidance, being still, eliminating distractions in my life, both physical and emotional, I started noticing them more and more. This is something that you will develop over time, but do not get discouraged. God wants us to get to our own Promised Land. He wants us walking in our purpose. It's what He created us to do in the first place. We have all been created for a purpose.

Proverbs 3:5-6 says, *"Trust in the Lord with all your heart, and do not lean on your own understanding. In all your ways acknowledge him, and he will make straight your paths."*

Psalm 32:8 says, *"I will instruct you and teach you in the way you should go; I will counsel you with my eye upon you."*

Another one of my favorite scriptures is in Isaiah 30:21, which says, *"And your ears shall hear a word behind you, saying, 'This is the way, walk in it,' when you turn to the right or when you turn to the left."*

Matthew 7:7-11 says, *"Ask, and it will be given to you; seek, and you will find; knock, and it will be opened to you. For everyone who asks receives, and the one who seeks finds, and to the one who knocks it will be opened. Or which one of you, if his son asks him for bread, will give him a stone? Or if he asks for a fish, will give him a serpent? If you then, who are evil, know how to give good gifts to your children, how much more will your Father who is in heaven give good things to those who ask him!"*

The last scripture I want to mention is in James 1:5-6 that says, *"If any of you lacks wisdom, let him ask God, who gives generously to all without reproach, and it will be given him. But let him ask in faith, with no doubting, for the one who doubts is like a wave of the sea that is driven and tossed by the wind."*

Pray for guidance and then listen. God will answer and guide you.

Journal Prompt: What are some breadcrumbs you've found, and what did they lead you to? If you can't think of any, what kind of simple breadcrumbs would you like to ask God to see?

STAY CONNECTED TO THE VINE

When I first encountered God in my bathroom a few years ago, one thing He said that really stood out to me was that my anxiety and feelings of depression and hopelessness were not coming as attacks from the devil as I thought. This really made me stop and think, "If this wasn't from the devil... where was it coming from?"

I've learned throughout my journey out of the valley that when I have a question about something, the best thing to do is first sit with that question in the presence of God and ask for clarity and guidance. The searching and reading comes later and is necessary, but before you dive right in and start trying to make sense of it, you'll be surprised at how quickly you can get a clear straight answer from our Creator and Lord.

When I sat in silence, asking God, "Why do I feel so terrible?" The answer started coming before I even finished my question. His answer was something like this, "You feel so terrible because you are straying away from me. Remain close to me and you will be restored and strengthened."

Hmmm. You don't say. "So I'm the problem this entire time?"

"Yes." I heard back from God.

This didn't surprise me, since at this point, I started realizing I was standing in my own way, causing more problems for myself because of fear, insecurity, control, pride, and approval of others. If I could learn to "Let go and let God," I would be great, but what did that even mean? I sat in silence first, took some time to write down the questions I had in my journal and then I began with a quick search online to find some of these answers in the Bible, and here's what I found.

"Letting go" means the control, the schemes, the plotting, the planning, the over-analyzing, the worrying, the doubting, the fear, and letting God solve the problem in His own way on His own timeline. All we have to do is our part of obedience which is to follow His instruction. In order to follow the instructions, we must learn what the instructions are and we tend to forget, especially as new believers, that all of the answers are in the Handbook of Life, AKA The Holy Bible.

So, let's take a look at what the scripture says about letting go. I searched "What does the Bible say about letting go?" and here's what I found:

Proverbs 3:5-6: *"Trust in the Lord with all your heart, and do not lean on your own understanding. In all your ways acknowledge him, and he will make straight your paths."*

Jeremiah 29:11: *"For I know the plans I have for you, declares the Lord, plans for welfare and not for evil, to give you a future and a hope."*

Isaiah 43:18-19: *"Remember not the former things, nor consider the things of old. Behold, I am doing a new thing; now it springs forth, do you not perceive it? I will make a way in the wilderness and rivers in the desert."*

1 Peter 5:7: *"Cast all your anxieties on him, because he cares for you."*

Matthew 6:33: *"But seek first the kingdom of God and his righteousness, and all these things will be added to you."*

Out of these scriptures, I realized that I need to first connect to God and then trust in Him, that He knows what He's doing, and that what He's doing will be a masterpiece.

Just like any relationship, the more time you invest in that relationship, getting to know the person, the closer you become and the more you know their voice, their intentions and their character. Spending time with Jesus is no different. If you want to get to know someone, spend your precious time with them.

But here's where most people go wrong: they're too busy. It's that simple. I was too busy to spend time with God because I had sales goals to hit, a promotion I was working towards, and I was drowning with responsibility inside my home. I didn't even have time to do the things I needed to do, I definitely didn't have time to sit down, relax and read my Bible or pray. I was in a hurry and I needed things to happen quickly, so I thought the more I worked, the quicker the success would come. WRONG.

If you don't have time to spend with Jesus, you will never feel fulfilled, you will never discover your purpose and walk in it, and you will spend the rest of your life craving abundance and joy, never finding it. "Nothing satisfies like Jesus," as my favorite coffee mug states. I had to learn this the hard way.

So, it's pretty simple; if you want to get to know Jesus, give Him your time and stay connected to Him. John 15:5 states, *"I am the vine; you are the branches. Whoever abides in me and I in him, he bears much fruit, for apart from me you can do nothing."*

I love the imagery of this scripture and the fruit vine. If you cut a bunch of grapes off from the vine before they were ripe, they would stop growing, wither and die, just like our lives and souls. We must stay connected to receive nourishment, care, and life in order to grow and prosper.

A very important way to stay connected to the vine is through a church. I know some of you reading this have been deeply hurt by your church and I want to apologize on behalf of all Christ-followers out there for what's been done to you and how it's made you feel. But you cannot let that keep you from the Christian influence you need. We are designed to be in community and to rely on others, but don't forget that the church is filled with real people who have real problems, who are hurt, have been through trauma, abandonment, and pain. Nobody is perfect other than Jesus, so it's extremely important that you don't put your faith in others, but instead always in Jesus.

The church is a great place to find like-minded Christians looking for similar things as you—joy, freedom, fulfillment, abundance, community, connection, purpose and answers. In the next chapter, we will learn more about the security team we need in place around us 24/7 in order to stay safe from the enemy, who is prowling around looking for someone to devour. But right now, I want you to understand the community aspect that's needed in order to grow. The church, the small group you attend, or the mentor you connect to. All of these people will help you strengthen your relationship with Christ in order to walk in freedom, abundance, and fulfillment daily.

When someone is in the valley, or when I find myself there, the first question I ask is "How much time have you spent 1-on-1 with Jesus in the last 7 days?" Chances are, if you're deep in the valley, you haven't been spending much time with Jesus at all. Maybe during the last few days, you have since you realized how awful you've felt, but usually it's because of our lack of time with Jesus that we begin falling down into the valley in the first place.

So, what can we do to ensure we do not stray away?

I use the acronym T.I.M.E to help me stay on track.

The "T" stands for thirty minutes. I have found that I need at least thirty minutes undistracted (this is key) to fully absorb God's presence and connect.

"I" stands for intimately. Although Youtube videos, sermons, and Christian audiobooks can be extremely helpful, it's not the same as spending time intimately with just you and Jesus. So, no other outside sources are allowed during this time except you, your Bible and God.

"M" stands for Mornings. Now, of course you can connect with God anytime, but mornings are the best time because you haven't begun your day yet. Your mind is focused and still, it's not racing with your never-ending to-do list yet. Also, mornings work best because you can't procrastinate and then run out of time. If you wake up and do this right away, then you will have done it right away. It's pretty simple.

Lastly, the "E" stands for Every Day. This is crucial; you need consistency. 1 Chronicles 16:11 says, *"Seek the Lord and his strength; seek his presence continually!"* The word "continually" is defined as: repeated frequently in the same way; regularly. Although meeting with God sometimes is better than never, continually is superior and is necessary. If you would like to learn more about spending T.I.M.E with God, listen to episode 40 from my WAKE UP! With Tarryn Sarcone Podcast found on Apple podcasts, Google podcasts, or Podbean.

Generational Blessings

Remember in the beginning of this book when we spoke about generational sins and curses and how they trickle down through your family lineage and wreak havoc? Well, the same can be true for generational growth and blessings. By focusing on spending T.I.M.E. with God, you will be paving the way for your future generations to do the same. Do not read only your Bible, pray, and spend time with God in your room with a locked door, but instead let your family see you connecting to God, for this is how they will learn. Children do as they see, not as they're told, so by them seeing you open your Bible in the mornings, journaling down your prayers and requests to God, and talking with Him, your children will be so much more likely to follow in your footsteps.

Teach them how to spend time with God in the morning before they start their day. A great way to do this is by being the role model they need and by showing them what you do. Imagine if your parents knew this stuff when you were little and they were devoted to linking with God to learn how to live and how to raise up their children. Imagine your mother or father reading their Bible and spending time deep in prayer every morning how different your life would've been. Imagine if they would've taught you how to connect with God, how to get to know him personally and intimately, and helped you memorize scripture that you could bury deep in your heart.

Instead, you're just learning this at age 25, 30, or 45. I'm not telling you this to discourage you, but instead to encourage you that there's no better time to start but right now. Start with these practices and show your children, or your future children, grandchildren, nieces, and nephews how to do this.

We only started doing this about a year ago. We created a brand-new routine in our home and instead of giving my girls tablets to watch as they fell asleep, we decided there would be no tablets around bedtime and instead each child could pick out three books, and then we would finish with the Bible. My husband and I divided to conquer the task and each night we would rotate who we read to swapping between girls. We thought there would be fights around the new routine, but there wasn't. We found that our girls loved spending quality time with us before bed instead of kids' Youtube videos, and so did we. This time became a time I looked forward to all day because I saw the opportunity to teach them. After we read the three books to each child that they would pick out, we would then read The Beginner's Bible until they fell asleep.

Reading this children's Bible was super helpful for me as a beginner reader as well, reading the stories that were easy to understand over, and over again each night, most nights I would find her sleeping and me deep in a story. I swear I learned more from reading that children's Bible for a few weeks than I had gotten from my adult Bible all my life.

Journal Prompt: Who has God strategically placed in your life that you can influence and teach them how to live their life connected to the vine? In what ways can you do this?

24/7 SECURITY

Iwanted to open this chapter by reading my favorite scripture, *"A Psalm of David. The Lord is my shepherd; I shall not want. He makes me lie down in green pastures. He leads me beside still waters. He restores my soul. He leads me in paths of righteousness for his name's sake. Even though I walk through the valley of the shadow of death, I will fear no evil, for you are with me; your rod and your staff, they comfort me. You prepare a table before me in the presence of my enemies; you anoint my head with oil; my cup overflows"* (Psalm 23: 1-6).

All of this The Lord does for us. He is constantly at work for us—guiding, directing, leading, correcting, and protecting. There isn't a single moment in our lives where He does not see us because He is a good Shepherd, taking care of His flock with a watchful eye. He wants us safe from the evil one in our lush green pastures, and that's exactly where you'd like to be as well, I'm guessing. Therefore, it is crucial that you are obedient and follow His instructions in order to receive protection from the evil one.

The Bible is filled with instructions on how to remain safe from the evil one, and a lot of those ways you have already learned by reading this book. Things like putting on your Armor of God, knowing your true identity, believing you have purpose, knowing you are anointed, and understanding generational curses and attacks. We also learned the importance of keeping your mind healthy and living a life free from sin by staying connected to the Father consistently.

We are His sheep and He is our Shepherd, protecting and guiding us to fresh water to drink and to green pastures for nourishment. But just like a sheep, in order to be cared for well, you must stay close to your Shephard.

In John 10: 9-10, Jesus says, *"I am the gate; whoever enters through me will be saved. They will come in and go out, and find pasture. The thief comes only to steal and kill and destroy; I have come that they may have life, and have it abundantly."*

Jesus so badly wanted us to have this full life that He came and laid down His own life for us, to protect us and to keep the enemy out. He didn't come for us to have a hard and miserable life, He came so that we would have an abundant life.

The enemy, Satan, is the thief. He's here to steal, kill, and destroy. He is very good at making Christianity look like a big disappointment filled with boundaries, disciplines, and limitations set for us. But these things aren't set for us to limit our lives and take away the fun like I used to complain about in my teenage years to my mom. Instead, they're there to protect us and save us from pain, hurt, heartache, loss, disappointment, and mistakes. Of course, in this life, we will experience pain and trials and loss, but we are able to avoid a lot of them by simply living a life as close to Jesus as we can.

Every time we sin, we are faced with consequences for our actions that rob us from the abundance God wanted. Now we serve such a faithful Shepherd that even when we mess up, Genesis 50:20 states, *"As for you, you meant evil against me, but God meant it for good, to bring it about that many people should be kept alive, as they are today."*

You've probably heard this scripture summarized as "what the enemy intended for evil, God will use for good." In this scripture we can see that the enemy's sole purpose is to harm us. He is the Father of all lies. He disguises himself as the angel of light, the deceiver of the whole world, and his personal name, "Satan," means "adversary." This name indicates Satan's basic nature: he is the enemy of God, of all God does, and of all God loves.

He prowls around like a lion, looking for someone to devour—looking for a sick, weak, or wandering sheep. The scripture comes from 1 Peter 5:8 and says, *"Be sober-minded, be alert. Your adversary the devil is prowling around like a roaring lion, looking for anyone he can devour."* That is why we must put on the full armor of God daily, be sober-minded and be alert.

Believing in God is simply not enough to fight against the schemes of the devil. In James 2:9, it says that even the demons believe in God and shudder, so just believing in God won't help.

Now hearing all of this might be a tad overwhelming to you, and you're probably pretty freaked out thinking of the spiritual war that is constantly going on around you. But I have great news! James 4:7 states, *"Resist the devil and he will flee."*

We also see in 1 Corinthians 10:13, *"No temptation has overtaken you that is not common to man. God is faithful, and he will not let you be tempted beyond your ability, but with the temptation he will also provide the way of escape, that you may be able to endure it."*

The purpose of this chapter is to show you how to remain safe.

Now that you are out of the valley and walking up the mountain towards the peak, the devil is going to be working overtime to get you back down into the valley where he thinks you belong. "The devil lets the sleeping dog lie" is a quote I had written on a sticky note and put on the window right in front of me in my office so that I could see it day after day. Now that you're "awake," he will not leave you alone until he knows you will not listen and tolerate him anymore.

It is so important we use every single tool we have to fight him because we have been given the tools to fight and win. The devil has already been defeated by God and has zero authority over our lives, so do not be tricked or deceived! You have to know the scriptures to recite when you feel fearful.

Colossians 1:3 says, *"He has delivered us from the domain of darkness and transferred us to the kingdom of his beloved Son."*

Ephesians 5:8 states, *"For at one time you were darkness, but now you are light in the Lord. Walk as children of light."*

Then in 1 John 4:4, we hear this encouraging message, *"Little children, you are from God and have overcome them, for he who is in you is greater than he who is in the world."*

Colossians 2:15 says, *"And having disarmed the powers and authorities, he made a public spectacle of them, triumphing over them by the cross."*

When I was first climbing out of the valley, I went through the Bible and wrote down as many scriptures as I could that showed God was in control and Satan was under my feet, desperate to never forget. You may have to do this too, but instead of studying your entire Bible, I made it easy for you and you can find all of my scriptures by visiting www.tarrynsarcone.com/TheValley. I highly recommend you print these out and put them somewhere you can see them and make a little note next to them that says "If I'm feeling fearful, worried, or doubting, read these!" This is going to be such a terrific reminder for you and will help you to fight off the devil's lies.

The last thing I want to mention when it comes to having 24-hour security is the importance of prayer. In Chapter 8: Rock Bottom, we discussed prayer being one of the offensive weapons God has given to us. As I stated in that chapter, we cannot neglect prayer, it's where we draw spiritual strength from God and it's also where we draw our protection.

Matthew 26:41 states, *"Watch and pray that you may not enter into temptation. The spirit indeed is willing, but the flesh is weak."* This right here is why we need to begin our day with prayer. We need to stay on guard and be alert for the enemy's schemes. I like to begin every day before I even get out of bed to ask God to protect me and guide me away from the evil one. I pray that He makes the enemy's plans known and that I am not deceived by him.

Before we move on to the next chapter, I want to remind you to not focus on doing any of this perfectly. You'll have periods in your life where you get distracted again and leave yourself open to attack. Micah 7:8 says, *"Do not rejoice over me, O enemy, though I fall I will rise; though I dwell in darkness, the Lord is a light for me."*

I also find comfort in Psalms 138:7: *"Though I walk in the midst of trouble, you will revive me. You will stretch forth your hand against the wrath of my enemies and your right hand saves me."*

Remember, there is nothing you can do to get God to abandon or forget you. He will always be there when you mess up and He's also already aware that you're going to. *"For we all sin and fall short of the glory of God"* (Romans 3:23).

The devil is going to try to use this against you when you sin and fall short. He's going to get in your head and make you feel dirty, unworthy, ashamed, guilty, and insecure. Every time I've seen people who are far from God, 100% of the time it's because they are keeping their distance from Him. He's waiting for you. You are not waiting on God to make a move.

This was one of the biggest revelations I had coming out of the valley. I kept complaining, saying how I was waiting on God to do things for me—to bring me success, to make me happy, to heal my mental health, and to mend my marriage, for starters. But it turns out, God was waiting for me. When you fully realize this and understand it, it really changes the way you move.

I wanted to share two parables from the Bible with you on this topic. The first one can be found in Luke 15:4-7 when Jesus told them: *"Suppose one of you has a hundred sheep and loses one of them. Doesn't he leave the ninety-nine in the open country and go after the lost sheep until he finds it? And when he finds it, he joyfully puts it on his shoulders and goes home. Then he calls his friends and neighbors together and says, 'Rejoice with me; I have found my lost sheep.' I tell you that in the same way there will be more rejoicing in heaven over one sinner who repents than over ninety-nine righteous persons who do not need to repent."*

The second is the parable of the lost son Jesus told that is recorded in Luke 15:11-24. *"There was a man who had two sons. The younger one said to his father, 'Father, give me my share of the estate.' So, he divided his property between them. Not long after that, the younger son got together all he had, set off for a distant country and there squandered his wealth in wild living.*

"After he had spent everything, there was a severe famine in that whole country, and he began to be in need. So, he went and hired himself out to a citizen of that country, who sent him to his fields to feed pigs. He longed to fill his stomach with the pods that the pigs were eating, but no one gave him anything.

"When he came to his senses, he said, 'How many of my father's hired servants have food to spare, and here I am starving to death! I will

set out and go back to my father and say to him: Father, I have sinned
against heaven and against you. I am no longer worthy to be called your
son; make me like one of your hired servants.' So, he got up and went to
his father.

"But while he was still a long way off, his father saw him and was
filled with compassion for him; he ran to his son, threw his arms around
him and kissed him. The son said to him, 'Father, I have sinned against
heaven and against you. I am no longer worthy to be called your son.'

"But the father said to his servants, 'Quick! Bring the best robe and
put it on him. Put a ring on his finger and sandals on his feet. Bring
the fattened calf and kill it. Let's have a feast and celebrate. For this son
of mine was dead and is alive again; he was lost and is found.' So, they
began to celebrate."

We can see by the words of Jesus in all of the scriptures mentioned
so far from this book, including the parables that He is head over heels
in love with you, will never leave you or forsake you. He is constantly
standing watch for you and keeping you safe but only if you stay in the
heard. If you isolate yourself and are all alone, there is no protection
and the devil will have his way with you. You are the Daughter of the
Highest King and your Daddy will win this battle, so stay close.

Journal Prompt: "What's one way that you are certain God has
protected you in life?"

TRIGGERS

"But the fruit of the Spirit is love, joy, peace, patience, kindness, goodness, faithfulness, gentleness and self-control..." Galatians 5:22.

These are the traits you exude as you get closer to Jesus and it's how a non-believer can tell you are a believer. But, however long you spend getting closer to Jesus, listening to His voice, reading his words and learning about your identity, you will still be triggered. We are human and we all experience emotion. Even Jesus himself experienced emotions like sadness, fear, and anger when He was here on earth as a human.

Somewhere in my life I developed the thought that showing emotions was a sign of weakness. I didn't believe people who showed emotions were weak, I only saw weakness in myself for displaying them. So, when I started going to therapy it took me a while to get comfortable with crying and letting out my emotions without a massive wave of guilt and shame to drown me afterwards. To be honest, this is still something I struggle with.

There is a difference between showing normal healthy emotions like stress, fear, pain, or sadness and being emotionally triggered. The biggest difference is that when you are emotionally triggered you don't necessarily understand why you're feeling a negative emotion, you just know you are. Most of the time, it seems to come out of absolutely nowhere. One minute you're fine, the next you're not. What happened?

Mood Swings

If you struggle with moods like me, you're going to want to start paying attention to your moods and what's happening around you, or what's being put inside of you when you're feeling good versus bad. How's your diet? Do you know that high amounts of sugar, caffeine, and processed foods can cause massive brain fog, irritability, and sleepiness? Try suffering with those symptoms and being put in charge of taking care of a baby, a couple toddlers, a pre-teen and having to run a household and be productive. Makes for one snappy mama, huh?

You need to put taking care of yourself and your own well-being at the top of your list. Don't eat healthy and move your body to lose weight, but do it to take good care of the blessing God has given you of health and life. You should be drinking half of your body weight in ounces of water each day, and if you're like me and the majority of the world and know you fall short of the nutrition you need on a daily basis, take a multivitamin, a probiotic, and some omegas. Consult with your doctor first, of course, and then I recommend you get on a good-quality supplement because where you buy them matters.

Let's talk about what's happening around you when you feel your mood decline. Are you triggered? Do you have poor boundaries and let people walk all over you, causing you to explode in anger? Maybe this has always been something you struggle with and you let other people's problems become your problems. Or maybe you feel your kids are completely out of control and you have no clue how to handle this phase you find yourself in. A book I recently read that helped me a lot in parenting was called *Triggers* by Amber Lia and Wendy Speake. I recommend getting a copy if this is something you struggle with.

Prayer is the number one thing you should be doing along with relying on God for change and help. This should not be your last resort. If you have received the Holy Spirit, then the old you is dead and gone, and the new you is here now. Pray daily and diligently that the Holy Spirit changes you and your moods once and for all. When we pray with desperation and conviction with bold audacity, God hears us. So, add this to your prayer list in your journal and make sure to recite this daily if moods are something you struggle with.

The last thing I want to mention about moods is medication. I am a huge advocate for natural healing and believe that the majority of things we take medication for as a society could be avoided with the proper diet and lifestyle changes, but sometimes our brains don't have what they need, and we need outside help. All I want to say is that if you've struggled with bad moods forever and it has become your full-time job to manage them and it's ruining your life, then maybe it's time to seek some professional help. You are not weak or taking the easy way out, you are simply giving your body and brain what it's lacking. So maybe it's a new supplement, diet, or medication. Add to your prayer list that God brings you whatever it is you need in order to help you heal.

Losing Control

Triggers usually cause some sort of irrational thinking or over-thinking, not allowing you to use logic, and your typical responses you would tend to have seem far away. For instance, you typically believe in gentle-parenting, trying not to raise your voice or say any harsh or negative words towards your children, but once the kids whining and constant fighting with each other will not stop, you find yourself growing a few feet taller, turning green and letting words come out of your mouth that you have no control over. Why are you out of control? Because you're triggered.

You can basically categorize all triggers into two main categories; internal and external triggers. The reason I have a chapter in the book on triggers is because this is something you will absolutely have to learn to overcome if you want to get into God's calling for your life. Healthy people still are triggered but they don't let those triggers cause a downward spiral right back into the valley. You will never be rid of triggers in your life, even if you were in a bubble and never left your home.

Once you identify the triggers you deal with mostly, you can become more aware and focused on them, allowing you to look up scriptures of what the Bible says about these topics, read books on the topics, and if necessary, get professional help.

For me, I knew I was triggered but I didn't know where it came from. This would cause me to overthink, over-analyze, doubt and question everything. I'd lose all belief in myself, feel overwhelmed and irritated, stressed and defeated. Within one minute I would go from the peak of a mountain, feeling on top of the world, crushing my goals and making a difference in my purpose, to sitting in the bottom of the darkest valley, feeling like my life was over.

At first, I thought I was crazy. Legitimately losing my mind. I had told my best friend, my husband and my mom about how I was feeling and asked if I should see a psychiatrist, be medicated, or admitted somewhere. Honestly. This is another reason I'm including this chapter on triggers because we are not crazy and we're not alone. Nobody talks about it, so it feels that way. I am talking about it. I am not going to allow you to feel like what's happening inside your mind—the triggers—make you feel crazy, because you are not. I am also not going to let the devil cause you to backslide down the mountain, not on my watch. You have done so much to pull yourself out of the valley, worked so hard... You aren't going back in that easily.

Triggers are things that you will have to slowly work on, pray over, and learn about. I don't think you will ever be able to get completely away from them, but you can learn to recognize them and then release them, or avoid them entirely.

Just the other day I found myself triggered, crying and feeling suffocated with my responsibilities and to-do list. I was spiraling into an anxiety attack, struggling to breathe, unable to think logically, and out of touch with reality.

So, when this happens, you need to ask yourself two questions: "Why do I feel like this?" and "What can I do in order to feel better right now?" You will have to understand *when* you started feeling like this in order to be able to answer the question. For me, I started feeling triggered when my sons asked me when we were going to do their homework and what was for dinner. I had just spent 5 hours staring at my computer screen updating my branding, my website, and planning content for the week. During this time, I felt great. I was listening to a playlist I loved, I was excited for all the changes I was making. I felt fulfilled and productive, a sense of relief for tackling this giant task on my to-do list and I felt creative and free. I get to work from my computer in my bed (my favorite place in my house to be), in comfy clothes, at home with no boss telling me what to do. This was my dream life, right? So, what happened?

Remember I talked about transitions in my Therapy chapter? This is something I had to seek professional help to learn, but for me, transitioning from one subject or category to another is triggering because my brain doesn't work well jumping from category to category, especially when each category has its own to-do list. So, when my son asked me about homework, that was triggering in itself because my brain was 100% focused on work. To answer his question, I had to pull myself out of work mode and look at my schedule and fit in a time for him.

All of this could've been avoided by the way by creating a proactive schedule instead of reacting to my day. Schoolwork is a top priority for me right now, so it is something that should be planned into every day before each day begins, that way everyone knows of the time that's blocked. There are no questions around it, and it will get done. That was my first mistake, and all we can do with our mistakes is learn from them and do better next time. Remember, progress over perfection. Even I struggle with this as I veer off the path occasionally.

This is when the Mom Guilt kicked in. Can you see the downward spiral?

The Mom Guilt was already present since my four-year-old spent most of the day playing by herself, watching movies and napping—all things that are completely fine for a four year old to do, by the way, especially since she wasn't left to entertain herself every single day and this was a one-off. But it didn't matter because I wasn't logically thinking about it. Instead, my emotions took over, making me feel like a terrible mom for ignoring and neglecting her all day, even though that was not true. Now I felt even worse for snapping on my son for asking me a simple question about dinner, causing my Mom Guilt to deepen.

I had about another half hour of edits to make on my website before I could publish the changes and I had to leave in an hour to go pick my nine-year-old up from school. So, I finished up the changes, I told my son homework would have to be done later and left to go pick up my daughter.

On the way, I called my husband, hoping he would offer some comfort and support by just reading my mind and catching my vibe. He answered and could immediately tell I was in a bad mood, but he had a stressful day at work himself and now was stuck in traffic on his way home from a work event. He asked, "What's wrong?" in a not-so-happy tone, which triggered me again. He was my safety, my person who was supposed to support me and make me feel better, but instead wasn't giving me the reaction I had come up with in my head that he was supposed to give and wasn't reading my mind like I had expected. All unrealistic expectations, by the way. I answered with "Nothing, never mind, I gotta go." I then hung up the phone and cried the entire way to the pickup line at school, wiping away my tears, rolling down the windows and hoping my daughter wouldn't notice something was wrong.

But during the couple of hours I was feeling overwhelmed and triggered, I had some choices I could make. I used to immediately reach for a drink of alcohol when I was triggered, calling a friend to go out for margaritas or pouring myself a glass of wine. When it wasn't alcohol, it was smoking weed—going out to the garage to hit a joint a couple of times hoping to calm down. For a while, when I cut alcohol out of my life for good, it became food I reached for, grabbing the container of Oreos or bag of chips that I would eat until the emotion went away. Isolation was also something I grasped when feeling triggered. I would not open up and talk to anyone about my problems, wouldn't communicate with my husband how I was feeling, and would just cancel all plans I could and avoid everyone at all costs, destroying my marriage.

Another huge thing you are going to want to avoid when triggered is scrolling on social media. This makes things so much worse for me, it's insane. When you are on your phone just scrolling and scrolling and scrolling, you are only adding more chaos to your brain—more stimulation, more comparison, and more thoughts... all things you need less of right now. So put down the phone, read, stretch or do a hobby you enjoy for a bit. People say they have no time, but they spend a lot of time each day on social media, don't get this twisted.

It's important to identify when a trigger begins so that you can avoid most from happening in the first place and learn from your mistakes. But not all triggers are avoidable, so it's important you learn how to handle triggers when they arise. We just learned not to reach for substances or things that will numb the emotion, but another thing you need to do is turn to Jesus.

On my drive to the school, I turned off the radio and spent the time crying and pouring my heart out to God, asking him to help me feel better, to allow the emotions to pass and to help my brain feel clear and light again. The scripture "Come to me all who are weary..." kept flooding into my mind, and I kept telling God I was weary and needed Him. Now, don't get too caught up in the words you need to say to God as you pray. Remember, He can understand what you need even with groanings and tears. He can read your mind and your heart. He knows and all you have to do is show up at His feet.

Once I got home, I knew I had failed myself with my lack of preparation and planning for the day, but it wasn't too late. I looked through the fridge and cabinets and decided we were ordering pizza, but I would also make a grocery list with our needs for the week in order to have dinners planned for the rest of the evenings that week, helping to avoid this from happening again. I also realized that I had not eaten anything since breakfast or drank any water today, consuming about a half pot of coffee while I worked, contributing to massive brain fog. This is another trigger for not only me but lots of women I talk with. When we neglect our own personal needs, we are triggered. We have to take care of ourselves in order to take care of others. We need water, and we need healthy food that will fuel us, and we need rest.

As I mentioned previously, all triggers can fall into an internal or an external trigger category. Some external triggers can be people, and this is a harder one to become aware of, especially if they're in your family and people you love. But you will know if someone is triggering you if when they're around you, they leave you feeling worse. If this is the case, remove yourself from the situation and set boundaries with the person, not allowing them in your space when you're vulnerable.

Most of my triggers lately are internal and are caused by not being in control, feeling rejection and fear popping up, Satan bringing up the past, questioning or worrying about the future and the list goes on and on. These can truly come out of absolutely nowhere and at times can feel impossible to overcome. When you're internally triggered, stop what you're doing, listen to something positive, fulfilling, and life-giving so that you can turn your brain off and focus on something else and remember this too shall pass. It's only coming from an emotion and all emotions pass eventually. If you're really desperate for relief and listening to something else isn't working, then go take a guilt-free nap.

Remember to match up your emotions with scripture. Feeling anxious? Look up scriptures that talk about anxiety. Feeling fearful?

Look up scriptures on what God says about fear. Don't just sit there wondering what God says on a subject—do the work yourself and read the scriptures out loud, letting the devil hear every single word.

So, the next time you're feeling triggered all of a sudden, ask yourself (and journal if you're able to) these questions:

1. Do I need to eat?
2. When was the last time I drank water?
3. Did I take my vitamins today?
4. When did I start feeling triggered? What was I doing?
5. Could this have been avoided? If so, how?
6. What are 20 things I am grateful for? (This helps to shift your brain to focus on something else.)
7. What topics can I look up scriptures on relating to this trigger?

THE KEY TO A FULFILLED LIFE

The entire purpose of writing and publishing this book is to inspire and teach you to take the steps necessary to get out of the valley, out of the devil's grip, and into your calling in order to experience fulfillment, joy, freedom and abundance. It's also to produce generational blessings into your lineage and to end generational curses and sin patterns. You have so much influence over the people in your life that by simply becoming a better version of yourself. You will raise the tide around you, allowing others to rise above more easily than you did.

You have a calling on your life. You have a purpose, God has a plan. He wants you on his team to help pull others out of darkness. He has a plan in all of your darkness and in all of your mess to turn things around and use your story for His good.

Don't allow yourself to be overwhelmed by this book and all the changes you need to make, because they're not all changes that you need to do alone. They are changes that are going to be done to you by God if you allow Him to work in your life and all you have to do is stay connected to Him. That's it. If you get one thing from this book it's to stay connected. Spend time every single day with God praying, reading His words in scripture, and learning from the Bible in order to grow closer to Him.

He wants you out of the valley more than you want to get out, just remember that. You're also His Daughter. He's head-over-heels in love with you. It's a love so deep and so wide, so infinite, and so unconditional that we can't even begin to wrap our minds around it because we've never known a love so pure, authentic and true from this world. If you stay connected to Him, you keep telling Him how you're feeling, you keep writing letters to Him in your journal, reciting the scriptures you've written down and staying connected to His people, you will do just fine. The tiny baby steps out of the valley will eventually add up and you'll look back and see your progress.

Keep re-reading this book, flipping to chapters that you need more than others during certain times, and little by little it will soak in. Keep this book on your desk or nightstand, or favorite in your Audible account so that you can see it and remember you have a plan and you are not alone.

You are no longer in the grips of the devil. Say out loud right now, even if it's a soft whisper, "Devil, you have held me long enough and I no longer believe in your lies. You have no authority over me and will no longer keep me from my calling. I know whose I am and what I was created for. I'm the Daughter of the Highest King who has been given authority to trample over you. Get beneath me where you belong and where you deserve!"

It is so important that I mention once you make it out of the valley and start walking up the mountain, you will go back down into the valley shortly after. I'm not telling you this to discourage you but to show you the truth so that you have realistic expectations. For the first year of intentionally trying to get out and live a life worthy of my calling, I would find myself sliding right back down into the valley days or even hours after getting out. So don't get discouraged if you find yourself still sitting in the valley after weeks of trying to climb out. Eventually, the time in the valley got less and less and the time for which I was able to stay out grew longer and longer.

Originally, I recorded a podcast episode stating that I didn't think it was possible to stay out of the valley forever because it had been over a year of trying my hardest to believe in who God said He created me to be, identifying my triggers and avoiding them, getting professional help through therapy and a 12-step recovery program that led me to sobriety. I was learning to identify and control my emotions, organize my life, live proactively, separate myself from toxic people, and distance myself away from things of this world and I still found myself in the valley more days than I would like to admit. I didn't think it was possible, but then it was.

It has been over three years now of focusing on the valley, and I can say that I still do visit the valley briefly each month, but it's usually based on my hormone cycle. I've learned to give myself much grace, compassion and love, not overthinking and over-analyzing the fact that I'm "not doing well." I say "visit" because that's exactly what it is. I'm there maybe 30 minutes to an hour max, and I'm able to get right back out.

I have learned to become super aware of the warning signs that let me know I'm headed to the valley so that I can catch myself falling before I get there and immediately use the steps to get back out.

Here at 12 warnings signs you are headed towards the valley:

1. Neglecting time with God.
2. Having lower than normal energy or feeling "run down" for no apparent reason other than being busy.
3. Unbalanced emotions such as feeling irritated, anxious, depressed or overwhelmed.
4. Being overly critical or judgmental to those around you that you love.
5. Feeling hopeless or worried about the future.
6. Feeling alone even though you're not.
7. Coping with your emotions through drugs, alcohol, food, shopping, etc.
8. Doubting what God's told you.
9. Being unorganized/living in clutter and chaos.
10. Living reactively instead of proactively.
11. Isolating/ avoiding commitments, relationships and/or responsibilities.
12. Having poor self-care.

I have created a step-by-step Valley Guide to help women in the valley easily take the first few steps they need to get out. You can download your free copy of the guide or share it with a friend in need by visiting www.tarrynsarcone.com/thevalley

I wanted to take this last chapter to sum up the main points that I made in this book by giving you my top tips to stay focused on:

1. Prioritize your life with God first and family second. All other responsibilities follow these two things. Don't forget that you have been strategically placed in your family, birth order, city, and community. If you have been blessed with children, it's because God wants you to prioritize that. He wants us to take good care of the things He has already blessed us with and in order to take care of something you must spend time nurturing it. Don't be too distracted by the business of this world. Remember to focus on the things that are important to God, not things that are important to the world. Get your entire family plugged into a church, spend time every day with God, and spend quality time with your children teaching them about God.

2. Separate yourself from toxic relationships. You can easily do this by praying God places a wedge between you and the toxic people in your life and replaces them with new Godly people who are uplifting, encouraging, and most importantly, point you towards God's word.

3. Take care of the temple God gave you aka your body. Are you getting enough sleep? Are you eating foods that will nourish your body and give you energy, reduce inflammation, and promote healing within the body? Are you drinking enough water and moving your body consistently? We've all heard the saying "you are what you eat" and this couldn't be more true. If you eat only junk, you will feel like junk. This also goes with the health of your mind, not just your physical body. Be careful what you allow to get into your mind—what you watch

on TV and what you listen to. The Bible says the eyes are the lamp to the soul because what you see is what you become. Fill your mind with positive affirmations, scriptures, uplifting and inspiring books, shows, and music.

4. Seek professional help whether it be a Christian counselor, 12-step program, a book, a small group class you enroll in through your church or online program. If you have experienced trauma, abandonment, or tragedy like the majority of people have, you need someone to hold your hand and walk through it. Do not just think you will grow out of it because you won't. You need to go back, walk through it and heal once and for all by rewiring and reprogramming your brain

5. Stay organized and proactive. Find a routine that works and feels good for you. Do you focus on planning your entire week in advance or one day at a time? Whatever it is, find it and stick to it. This will allow you to move quicker and be lighter on your feet instead of being weighed down by unnecessary stress and thought.

6. Recite scriptures about your identity often so that you do not forget who you were created to be. Remember you are chosen & anointed to do big things. If you need the constant reminder like I do, purchase any of my Chosen & Anointed apparel found at www.tarrynsarcone.com/thevalley

7. Find your purpose and don't stop until you do. Finding your purpose can take some time to do. What are you good at? What are your talents? What are your natural gifts God has given you and how can you use them to further the kingdom? We have all been given gifts and talents that align with our purpose on earth. You're reading this book because you know you have purpose and that there has to be more to this life,

but you're probably not sure what that is. If you're desperate to tap into that and learn what on earth you're here for, check out my online course that helps women just like discover their purpose by visiting www.mentoringthemasses.com

You no longer are a slave to the valley or need to fear it. You have Jesus, you have power, you have authority and you have purpose. You are chosen, anointed, special, set apart, unique, and exceptional. You no longer have to walk in darkness ever again.

"Jesus spoke to the people once more and said, 'I am the light of the world. If you follow me, you won't have to walk in darkness, because you will have the light that leads to life" (John 8:12).